I0802363

Spring Training *in* Clearwater

SPRING TRAINING *in* CLEARWATER

Fencebusters and Fastballs from the Philadelphia Phillies and the Clearwater Threshers

Alejandro M. de Quesada

Foreword by Larry "The Baron" Shenk

Charleston London
History
PRESS

Published by The History Press
www.historypress.net

Front cover: Bobby Wine at the newly constructed Carpenter Field. In the distance is U.S. Highway 19. Wine played for the Phillies from 1960 to 1968. Carpenter Field was built in 1967 as an additional training facility. *From the Collection of AdeQ Historical Archives.*
Back cover: A scene from behind the Threshers' dugout during pregame warm-ups before a game against the Sarasota Reds, 2006. *Photo by the author.*

First published 2007
Manufactured in the United States

ISBN 978.1.59629.214.7

Library of Congress Cataloging-in-Publication Data

De Quesada, A. M.
Spring training in Clearwater : fencebusters and fastballs from the Philadelphia Phillies and the Clearwater Threshers / Alejandro M. de Quesada.
p. cm.
Includes bibliographical references.
ISBN-13: 978-1-59629-214-7 (alk. paper)
1. Spring training (Baseball)--Florida--History. 2. Philadelphia Phillies (Baseball team)--History. I. Title.
GV875.6.D42 2007
796.357'6409759--dc22
2006038514

To my daughter, Caroline Grace de Quesada,
whose love for the game and for her favorite
team inspired me to write this book.

Contents

Foreword

Hundreds of players have worn a Phillies uniform in spring training, from Kyle Abbott to Jon Zuber. Hall of Famers from Richie Ashburn to Robin Roberts to Jim Bunning to Mike Schmidt called Clearwater home in the spring. By Saam and Harry Kalas, two Hall of Fame announcers, broadcast games to millions of fans. Allen Lewis, Ray Kelly Sr. and Bus Saidt, writers also in Cooperstown as winners of the Spink Award, wrote many a story from Clearwater.

When Pete Rose was in camp with the Phillies his first spring (1979), we had to rope off left field to make room for fans to stand. More sea gulls than usual seemed to be there that day.

We had an outfielder named Ron Stone who hit so well in Clearwater we nicknamed him "Palm Tree." Once he got back North, the bat didn't produce as it had done down here.

I remember Bill White trying to come back from an Achilles tendon injury late in his career. He tried to do too much too soon and re-injured himself while taking ground balls. I can still see him lying face down on the clubhouse floor at Jack Russell Stadium saying, "You dummy, you dummy."

There was an infielder named Mike Buskey who was in camp in the mid-1970s, his only Major League camp. He got released and asked to use my telephone. I stood outside my office but overheard him: "Mom, I got released today. I don't have any money. Can you send me some money?"

There was a young pitcher named Lowell Palmer in the previous decade. Pitching mounds were located under the stands at Jack Russell Stadium. If it rained, pitchers could still get their throwing in on these mounds. Palmer could throw hard. You could hear the catcher's mitt—pop! pop!—when he threw. Manager Gene Mauch, in his famous pose of standing with his arms crossed over his chest, mumbled, "With stuff like that, he'll never lose." Unfortunately, that prediction fell short as Palmer was 5–18 in parts of five big league seasons.

Players who used to visit Clearwater in the spring now call this area home. Many instructors have done the same and some alumni have retired here.

Back in the 1940s, the Phillies were part of the community during a very small window in March. Today, the Phillies have a year-round relationship with Clearwater.

As a young Phillies fan growing up in central Pennsylvania in the 1950s, there was nothing like hearing the first radio broadcast from Clearwater. It brought warm thoughts of spring and summer. Winter woes would soon be gone. Hearing games from Jack Russell Stadium, one could only imagine what the place looked like. (Yes, there was television back then, but spring training games were not on the tube.) It never entered my mind that one day I would be working for the Phillies and falling in love with Clearwater.

As a rookie in 1964, I was in heaven watching my heroes at Jack Russell, which had to be converted into a Major League baseball infield every spring by the city of Clearwater. The stadium was home to the Clearwater Bombers, a professional softball team that seemed to be more popular with the natives than the Phillies.

The press box was an open-air area at the top of the stands behind home plate. Pigeons roosted in the steel beams. A daily chore was cleaning their friendly droppings. Spring training games didn't draw many fans back then. I remember carrying complimentary tickets to give to fans.

Once a player was cut from the big league roster, he was sent to Dade City or Leesburg in central Florida. I don't remember the specifics, but Class A players trained in one city and AA and AAA in the other.

Paul Owens, the farm director at the time, convinced the Carpenter family, who owned the Phillies, to build a training complex in Clearwater for the minor league players. Carpenter Field opened in 1967. The Phillies placed a Class A team in the city in 1985, the Clearwater Phillies, now the Threshers. In 1999, they added a team at Carpenter Field in the Gulf Coast League, a rookie league that plays from June until the end of August. Beautiful Bright House Networks Field, adjacent to Carpenter Field, opened in 2004. Without a doubt, the Phillies have the best spring training setup in Florida.

Some fans vacation there to escape the winter weather. For those back North, Clearwater datelines appear in newspapers and spring training games are broadcast on radio and television all across the Delaware Valley. Internet broadcasts go worldwide. For everyone—fans, players, staff and media—there's nothing like spring training in Clearwater, the true winter home of the Phillies.

Larry Shenk
Vice-president, Public Relations
Philadelphia Phillies Baseball Club

Introduction

Baseball is a gigantic part of our culture and our psyche. When the game is mentioned, one imagines trying to eat a hot dog with every conceivable condiment; the vendor shouting, "Peanuts, beer and Cracker Jacks!"; kids of all ages crowding along the dugout to seek autographs and photos of their favorite players; and checking out the team's new prospects. But the most incredible aspect of experiencing the game is the lifetime memories we create. These memories bind us together and are the reason why baseball is more than just a game—it is our heritage.

I was lucky to have grown up in the Tampa Bay area because it was the spring training home for several Major League teams. Baseball was everywhere. I remember going with my father and brother to the spring training games at Al Lopez Field in Tampa and watching players such as Johnny Bench and Pete Rose of the Cincinnati Reds play against Mike Schmidt and Tug McGraw of the Philadelphia Phillies. One memorable game was when my father lost us after we left the stadium. Upon finding my brother and I, he informed us that President Reagan had been shot. I still have the photos that were taken during the game.

Living in Culbreath Isles in the 1970s, the local rumor was that Pete Rose had a house behind my parents'. I'm sorry to say that rumor was not substantiated; however, we did have quite a few foul balls going over the wall into that backyard of the house in question. The local kids had my little brother Carlos and me go over to reclaim the balls, in order to find out who lived in the house. An elderly lady greeted us at the door with the balls in hand, and before we could interrogate her, she handed over the balls and closed the door. My brother and I still told our friends that we met Pete Rose's mom as a means of saving face. We became five-minute celebrities! In addition, almost every day on the way home from school, we used to pass a hotel on the corner of Kennedy and West Shore Boulevard, where there was a large banner proclaiming it the Spring Training Home of the Cincinnati Reds.

But when spring training ends in Tampa Bay, it necessarily does not end the baseball season. The minor league teams that are affiliated with the Major League teams begin moving into the spring training facilities and stadiums. In the 1970s and 1980s, I enjoyed watching my favorite team, the Tampa Tarpons, play against other teams such as the St. Petersburg Pelicans. The games ran through the summer and were a great escape from the long, hot and lazy summer days. In those days, my parents would drop off my friends, my brother and me with a couple of dollars for drinks, hot dogs and souvenirs, picking us up afterward when they were through shopping at the adjacent mall. In the car we would brag about who we saw, trade baseball cards, recount events from the game and show off the foul balls we had caught. I cherished those childhood memories, particularly those when I just hung out with my dad and brother at Al Lopez Field. Going the way of most things of the past, Al Lopez Field was razed to the ground in 1989. Only the memories live on.

During the mid- to late 1990s, over a decade later, when I began working on *Baseball in Tampa Bay*, I started visiting all the spring training facilities within the Tampa Bay area. My daughter, Caroline, would join me and watch the games in various stadiums. Though she still hadn't developed a love and understanding for the game at the time, she had developed an appreciation for hot dogs, cracker jacks and large sodas found at the stadiums. When she was off school for the summer, she was particularly fond of watching the Tampa Yankees (Legends Field), the St. Petersburg Rays (Al Lang Field), the Dunedin Blue Jays (Grant Field), the Lakeland Tigers (Marchent Stadium) and the Clearwater Phillies (Jack Russell Stadium). By 2004, with the opening of Bright House Networks Field, the spring training home of the Philadelphia Phillies and the home of the Clearwater Threshers, my daughter and I had adopted the Clearwater baseball facility as our choice for watching games. In the years since, Caroline's interest in baseball, especially anything relating to the Phillies and the Threshers, has become obsessive. Since 2005, she has participated in the Threshers Baseball Summer Camp and has

The author in Bright House Networks Field at the beginning of the 2006 Clearwater Threshers baseball season. *Photo by Caroline de Quesada.*

received season tickets for her birthday. I would have to admit that I have been a contributing factor in her "phanaticism" for the game. Caroline's greatest thrill was to be an announcer during the third inning in a game between the Clearwater Threshers and the Fort Myers Miracles on August 29, 2006.

While the players are the main attraction during spring training and during the minor league baseball season, in my opinion it is those who work behind the scenes who make the whole experience at Bright House Networks Field unbelievable. These stellar contributions are from people such as Opie Cheek, who makes sure that the playing field is well manicured and presentable; Chris Guckian, who greets fans at Diamond Outfitters with a smile and whose husband serves as an announcer for the games; and Carrie Jenkins-Adams and Amanda Warner, who together make sure that special events run smoothly during the game and oversee programs—such as the Li'l Anglers Club and the Threshers Summer Baseball Camp—that cater to children. It was here that Carrie met and married her co-worker, Jason Adams. These people and many others make the fans feel welcomed and appreciated by the Phillies. Because of these hardworking staff members, Bright House Networks Field is a place where families can be entertained at various levels and makes fans yearn to return.

Following the history of baseball in Tampa Bay, I've found the Phillies the most interesting because of their long association with both Clearwater and Pinellas County. Spring training in Clearwater began in the 1920s, and it was here that many players, such as Al Lopez, got their start in the Major Leagues. Many famous players came through Clearwater for spring training games, such as Babe Ruth, Lou Gehrig, Bob Feller and Robin Roberts. Though the Phillies and the sparkling city of Clearwater have had a love affair for many years, at the beginning, the team was a spurned suitor. In 2007, as the Phillies mark their sixtieth year of spring training in Clearwater and the twenty-second year of their minor league affiliate, it is fitting to review the spring training history of the city and the teams.

Spring Training's Early Beginnings

The earliest baseball teams that came to Pinellas County for spring training initially gathered at the ballpark established near Coffee Pot Bayou in St. Petersburg. After much negotiation and concessions made with the city and the team, the St. Louis Browns arrived in St. Petersburg on February 16, 1914. Ten days after the arrival of the team, the citizens were able to watch a game between the Browns and the Cubs (then training in Tampa).

In 1915 the Philadelphia Phillies replaced the Browns and called St. Petersburg their spring training home for the next three years. Pat Moran, the Phillies manager, began to set up some new rules for his players. All the players had to walk the two miles from their hotel to the ballpark and back. According to Rich Wescott, "Practice consisted of morning and afternoon sessions, with the hotel delivering lunch that often featured horrible tasting fish with heads still intact. [The meal was possibly smoked mullet—a Floridian delicacy and usually an acquired taste for Northerners.] Players often dumped the fish and picked oranges for their lunch. Once in a while, roast beef was served, but that was wholly unappetizing, too, as Grover Alexander ably demonstrated when he removed a piece from his sandwich and nailed it to the sole of his shoe."

Moran drilled his players in baseball fundamentals day in and day out during their spring training in Pinellas County. He maintained a strict discipline amongst his players and did not tolerate those who strayed from his rules. The coach was the first to introduce specific hand signals for use by the pitchers and catchers. Moran

> *also had his players endlessly practicing cutoffs, breaking up double plays, throwing to second and third on bunts, and working on plays in different situations. The pitchers were drilled on pickoffs, covering first base, and backing up other bases, and they were taught to keep records on opposing hitters. During a game, everybody on the bench had a specific job, whether it was trying to steal the other team's signs, noting the traits of the opposing pitcher, or observing the habits of the enemy hitters. Once, when Rixey spent too much time fooling around on the bench instead of watching the rival pitcher, Moran strolled over and rapped a fungo bat across his toes.*

The first Major League team to train in Clearwater was the Brooklyn Dodgers, first arriving in 1923, when the city's population was about three thousand. By the time the Dodgers left after the 1932 spring training session, the population had grown to about ten thousand. One of the great minor league teams of all time—the Newark Bears of the International League—replaced the Dodgers for three years, but Brooklyn returned in 1936 and stayed through 1941. In both 1931 and 1941, the Dodgers started their training in Havana, then came to Clearwater.

In 1908 Charles Ebbetts had gained full control of the Brooklyn franchise and built a stadium for the team in Brooklyn, opening as Ebbets Field in 1913. Ebbetts was influential in bringing the Brooklyn team down south for spring training and chose Clearwater as his Florida base of operations in 1923. As stated in Glenn Stout's *The Dodgers*, when Charles Ebbetts arrived in Clearwater for spring training and to seek real estate opportunities in 1925, "he thought nothing of dropping a quarter of a million dollars on a land deal to build a hotel, then fell ill. Eschewing his Brooklyn home, he returned to his hotel suite at Manhattan's Waldorf Astoria, where he was too weak to leave his bed. Ebbetts didn't make it through the first season week of the Dodgers' season. He died on 18 April of heart disease."

During the years when the Brooklyn Dodgers trained in Clearwater, numerous rookies arrived for their first spring training, among them Alfonso Ramon Lopez. As recounted in Wes Singletary's biography of the player, Al Lopez remembered how his manager, Wilbert Robinson, took him under his wings and his paternal treatment of the young players: "He was a nice man; like a father to me. He treated me real nice and he wanted me to sit next to him my first year when I started catching in

1930. Just sit there and we'd talk things over. He'd watch the ballgame and I'd sit next to him—learning." Lopez came out of spring training and it was noted in the press of the day that "Alfonso Lopez, twenty-eight-year-old Spaniard," would be ready to play with the Dodgers for the 1930 baseball season. He was actually twenty-one and had already been playing professional baseball for five years! The defensive abilities Lopez displayed in the minors were clearly his most valued, even though most observers of the time thought his bat was ready for the challenge as well. The speculation fell toward the high side as to how many games Lopez might catch. Al's stamina was unquestioned when he caught 143 games the previous summer in the Southern League. Lopez's first game was on April 27 against the New York Giants.

"El Señor," as Al Lopez was known, set numerous records over his long career in baseball. His achievements included most career games caught in the Major Leagues (1,918), most years catching 100 or more games in the National League (twelve) and most games caught without a passed ball in the National League (114). He led National League catchers in fielding average four times, and in assists four times. Following his retirement as a player, Al Lopez embarked upon a seventeen-year managerial career, which included two American League pennants and ten second-place finishes. His teams finished out of the first division only three times in seventeen years, giving him the ninth highest winning percentage in baseball history (.584). In 1959 his American League champion Chicago White Sox—known as "the Go-Go Sox" because of their penchant for running wild on the bases—stole 113 bases, 45 more than the second-place team. After retiring to Tampa following the 1969 season, he was later named to the Baseball Hall of Fame in 1977. El Señor passed away in Tampa on October 30, 2005.

While not practicing baseball skills at their spring training facility, many of the Dodgers' other players, coaches and managers over the years found various means of distraction while staying within the Tampa Bay region. Dazzy Vance and Edward Alexander were known to go off and fish in the waters of Clearwater. Some such as Al Lopez and Babe Ruth would play golf in the many golf courses scattered around the Tampa Bay area. Lopez's Brooklyn Dodgers teammate, Manuel Onis, recounted in Singletary's biography of Lopez how he and Al would play golf during the off-season: "Al and I spent the winter playing golf at Macfarlene Park, in West Tampa. The city had a nine-hole golf course there. You only needed to use an iron, a putter, and a pitching wedge. That's all it took."

It was during Brooklyn's years in Clearwater that the name "Dodgers" was emblazoned across the front of both the home and road uniforms in block letters in 1933. In 1938 the accent color was changed to royal blue.

From 1939 until 1945, the team had "Brooklyn" across the front of the road uniform in script letters. Interestingly, it was the Cleveland Indians who put numbers on their uniforms' sleeves in 1916 and the New York Yankees that were the first to put large numbers on the back of the uniform in 1929.

The Cleveland Indians came to Clearwater in 1942 and returned in 1946 after the wartime restrictions that had prevented any teams from going south for the intervening three years were lifted. During World War II, baseball was not a priority, but the entertainment it provided was deemed important by President Franklin Delano Roosevelt. On January 15, 1942, the president issued the "Green Light" letter and informed Baseball Commissioner Kenesaw Mountain Landis that the 1942 Major League baseball season should proceed. FDR felt that continuing professional baseball during wartime was good for America's morale. However, injuries and military service decimated the rosters of many Major League teams, including those of the Cleveland Indians.

In *Legends of the Tribe*, Morris Eckhouse describes this phenomenon:

> *Cleveland, with its loss of Bob Feller, and Detriot, with its loss of Greensberg, were arguably the two teams hit hardest in 1942 by the entry of the United States into World War II. Jim Bagby Jr., acquired from the Red Sox after the 1940 season, came up as the ace pitcher for the Indians, winning 17 games. Harder added 13 victories. Les Fleming took over from Trosky at first base and led the team with a .292 batting average, 14 home runs and 82 RBI...Lou Boudreau could count on himself and little else for the 1942 season. He was classified 4-F due to a pair of bad ankles. Familiar faces Mel Harder, Al Smith and Al Milnar returned to the pitching staff. Boudreau's double-play partner, Ray Mack, was back along with Ken Keltner at third.*

In addition, many teams suffered at the gate in 1942, and Cleveland was hit the hardest with a sharp decline of 40 percent to 459,447. As a concession to the wartime needs, teams began to train closer to their homes between 1943 and 1945. Cleveland moved to Purdue University in Lafayette, Indiana, for spring training during the war years.

The year before World War II, a girls' softball team called Peggy's Girls formed in Clearwater and played throughout the war. The team had made it to the Women's Softball Championship in Chicago in the late 1930s. When men went off to fight in World War II, many women entered professional baseball when the All-American Girls Professional Baseball League (AAGPBL) was formed. The women kept baseball alive at a time when public interest would have waned because of the war. Eventually, training camps for the league were established in Havana, Cuba, and in Fort Lauderdale, Florida. The AAGPBL ceased to exist after 1954, but there was an increase in the public's awareness of women's role in baseball because of the 1992 film *A League of Their Own*. A permanent exhibit highlighting the role of women in baseball now stands in the Baseball Hall of Fame.

With the end of World War II, many baseball players who had volunteered for military service began to be discharged from the armed forces in the winter of 1945 and early 1946. Bob Feller's first full season after returning from World War II was his best. Winning 26 games, his 348 strikeouts were a career high and his 2.18 ERA was a career low. He pitched his second no-hitter on April 30, 1946, a 1–0 win over New York at Yankee Stadium. With the exception of Bob Feller, the mass return of war veterans into the Major Leagues during the 1946 baseball season resulted in a forgettable 68–86 campaign for the Cleveland Indians.

Before leaving Clearwater in 1946, the Indians announced they would return in 1947, but the club was sold that June to the late Bill Veeck, a war veteran and savvy baseball marketer. Soon after the sale a note appeared in the *Sporting News* that revealed Veeck was considering having the Indians train the following spring in Tucson, Arizona, where he owned a ranch and had begun to restore some luster back to his newly acquired baseball franchise. Veeck's first full season as owner in 1947 dawned with a new optimism, a new team image in the form of a team logo and a new spring training site: Tucson, Arizona. New uniforms had been introduced in 1946—the first substantial change to Cleveland's home uniforms since 1929. The 1946 home jerseys featured "Indians" in red script with navy blue trim, replacing the large red wishbone "C." In addition, a patch commemorating the 150th anniversary of the city of Cleveland was worn on the left sleeve. Then in 1947, the animated face of an Indian sporting a toothy grin was added to the left shoulder. "Chief Wahoo" was now a part of Cleveland baseball and over time became increasingly controversial.

Paul Ficht, secretary of the Clearwater Chamber of Commerce, read the note in the *Sporting News* and contacted Veeck, who asked for time to make a decision over whether he would move the team. Others read the note, too, and four other clubs contacted the city and indicated interest if the Indians left. The four were the St. Louis Browns, who trained from 1925 through 1927 in nearby Tarpon Springs, and had been unhappy in 1946 when they worked out in Anaheim, California; the Philadelphia Phillies; and two New York Yankees farm clubs, Newark and Kansas City. When Veeck announced that the Indians would train in Tucson, Ficht, Mayor J.C. House, City Manager F.L. Hendrix and other city officials conferred and decided the Browns, American League pennant winners in 1944, would be the most desirable of the four. They figured the Browns would draw the most fans to the exhibition games and the most visitors from the North.

Hendrix wired Browns General Manager Bill DeWitt an invitation to open negotiations for a contract, but got no response. DeWitt was quoted in St. Louis as saying that the Browns had received an offer to train in Miami, but made no mention of Clearwater, then a city of over twenty thousand. At that point, Clearwater contacted the Phillies and on July 27, F.L. Hendrix announced that the Phillies and owner Bob Carpenter had accepted Clearwater's invitation to train there in 1947.

Since the end of the Civil War, baseball has become more and more popular throughout the United States. Seen here are members of a Clearwater baseball team at the turn of the twentieth century. Local teams would don women's clothing or similiar stunts as a means of attracting crowds to the games. *Courtesy Pinellas County Historical Museum.*

Pinellas County formally separated from Hillsborough County in 1912 and soon after local baseball teams were raised. This Clearwater baseball team posed for this photograph around 1914. On some of the players' shirts are the letters "PC" for Pinellas County. *Courtesy Pinellas County Historical Museum.*

A crowd of baseball fans watching a game between the Philadelphia Phillies and the St. Louis Browns at the Waterfront Field in St. Petersburg in 1915. Even though the Phillies trained in Pinellas County for a short period during World War I, the team would eventually return following World War II and play one of the longest roles in Clearwater's baseball history. *Courtesy Pinellas County Historical Museum.*

The Clearwater Board of Trade holds a baseball demonstration to help promote baseball in Clearwater in May 1922. A relocated Florida state franchise team called the Daytona Beach Islanders arrived in Clearwater in 1924 and renamed themselves the Clearwater Pelicans. *Courtesy Tampa-Hillsborough County Public Library System.*

By the 1920s, baseball had become a national pastime throughout the United States and abroad. Children became fascinated with the sport and schools began to form teams to play against each other. Seen here are members of the Clearwater High School baseball team that consisted of lads from Clearwater and nearby Dunedin during the Roaring Twenties. Interestingly, Dunedin did not have a high school until the 1960s, so the young boys from Dunedin played in Clearwater uniforms. The "CW" on the uniform appears backward because the negative was reversed at the time that this photograph was printed. *Courtesy Dunedin Historical Museum.*

Grant Field, located on the corner of Douglas and Beltrees, was dedicated to A.J. Grant and is shown here as it appeared in the 1930s. The field was built as a WPA government project to provide work for young unemployed men during the Depression. The complex has undergone numerous improvements and now hosts the Toronto Blue Jays and their affiliate Florida State League team. The field is literally a stone's throw from Clearwater city limits. *Courtesy Dunedin Historical Museum.*

The Brooklyn Dodgers used Clearwater as a base for their spring training between 1923 and 1932 and again between 1936 and 1940. Seen here is an image of the team while in Clearwater in 1926. *Courtesy Pinellas County Historical Museum.*

The Dodgers are pictured here in their spring training camp in Clearwater during the late 1920s. Wilbert Robinson (seated at center, in a suit) served as the manager for the Brooklyn Dodgers. *Courtesy Florida State Archives.*

A collage of Al Lopez and Dolfe Luque of the Brooklyn Dodgers with signed baseballs taken on August 17, 1931. Lopez, a local boy from the Hispanic communities of Ybor City and West Tampa, became one of Tampa Bay's best-known and most loved ballplayers. *Courtesy Tampa-Hillsborough County Public Library System.*

Like any place throughout Florida, Clearwater offered many opportunities for players to take time off from spring training and find worthwhile and relaxing activities. Seen here are Dazzy Vance (with fish) and Edward Alexander (with fishing rod) taking a break from baseball on December 23, 1931. *Courtesy Tampa-Hillsborough County Public Library System.*

Beginning in 1925, Al Lopez began playing for the Tampa Smokers, and by 1931 he was playing for the Brooklyn Dodgers. He was one of the few Hispanics who would enter into professional baseball in the early part of the twentieth century. *Courtesy National Baseball Library.*

From time to time, the New York Yankees' Babe Ruth would play against the Dodgers in Clearwater during spring training exhibition games and would even go off golfing and fishing in the area when time permitted. He is seen here with Al Lopez and fellow Dodgers teammate Van Lingle Mungo, a right-handed pitching star for the team, in the 1930s. *Courtesy* La Gaceta.

A relic from the past, a ticket stub for one of the spring training games in Clearwater during the 1940 season. *From the Collection of AdeQ Historical Archives.*

When the men went off to fight in World War II, many women entered baseball when the All-American Girls Professional Baseball League was formed. The women kept baseball alive at a time when public interest would have waned because of the war. A permanent exhibit highlighting the role of women in baseball now stands in the Baseball Hall of Fame. Twin sisters Mary and Myra Crisman were very involved in athletic activities in Pinellas County. Here, the pair is dressed in their softball uniforms for the Clearwater team Peggy's Girls. This team would participate in the Women's Softball Championship in Chicago in the late 1930s. *Courtesy Dunedin Historical Museum.*

The Cleveland Indians replaced the Brooklyn Dodgers in 1942; however, with the outbreak of World War II, they were not able to return to Clearwater until 1946. Seen here is Cleveland Indians outfielder Bob Lemon. Lemon played for the Indians from 1941 to 1942 and from 1946 to 1958. He was named to the National Baseball Hall of Fame in 1976. Following the spring training season in 1946, the teams moved their spring training camp to Tucson, Arizona, for the following season. *From the Collection of AdeQ Historical Archives.*

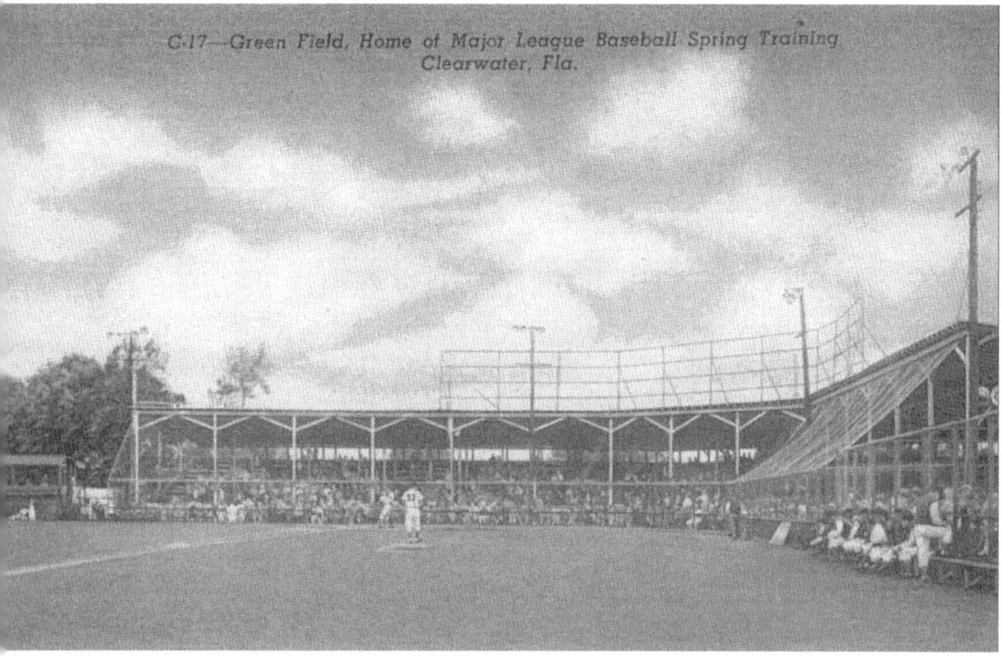

From the 1920s to the 1940s, Green Field had been the spring training home from the Brooklyn Dodgers to the Cleveland Indians. The field was fast becoming antiquated, however, and in 1947 new tenants would arrive and change the face of spring training in Clearwater in the decades to come. *From the Collection of AdeQ Historical Archives.*

The Phillies Come to Town

The Phillies—who had trained in Miami Beach in 1941, 1942 and 1946—had only a one-year deal when they held their first workout in Clearwater on February 24, 1947, but soon Phillies Traveling Secretary Nathan "Bebe" Alexander opened negotiations with city officials for a long-term contract. This came on the heels of a report that the Indians were unhappy in Arizona and might want to return to Clearwater. On March 7, the Phillies and the city of Clearwater signed a ten-year deal that would keep the Phillies in Clearwater, and four days later Mayor Houze threw out the first ball before three thousand fans as the Phillies opened their first exhibition season in Clearwater at the Clearwater Athletic Field.

Before the arrival of the Philadelphia Phillies, all the pro teams, starting in 1923, had used the old field. Home plate was located on Pennsylvania Avenue, which ran south to north along the third base line, near Seminole Street. Left field ran parallel to Palmetto Street, and right field ran parallel to Greenwood Avenue. The distance to the left field corner was 340 feet, but it was only 290 feet to the right field corner. A wooden fence enclosed the park and a high wire screen, requested by the Indians at the end of their 1946 training, topped the right field fence. There was a wooden clubhouse beyond third base and wooden stands seated three thousand. In their first exhibition as the home team in Clearwater, the Phillies lost to the Detroit Tigers, 13–1. In fact, the Phillies dropped their first seven games against big league opposition and posted their only home win that spring on March 28. That day they edged the St. Louis Cardinals, 8–7, when outfielder Johnny Wyrostek homered in the ninth inning and again in the eleventh. The Phillies' attendance of 13,291 that spring was ninth among ten Florida communities that had hosted Major League clubs for spring training. Still, the club and city were happy with each other, and have remained that way ever since.

The following spring, future Hall of Famer Robin Roberts recounted his first day in Clearwater:

> *My first spring training was 1948 with the Phillies in Clearwater, Florida…I flew down to Florida to join the Phillies at spring training. After landing at the airport in Tampa, I took a cab over the causeway to Clearwater. It had been snowy and cold in Michigan, but the weather was beautiful when I arrived in Tampa. I thought I had died and gone to heaven with the beautiful weather and blue water everywhere. I checked in at the Phoenix Hotel in Clearwater and was assigned a room. Later in the day I met my first roommate, Richie Ashburn. That spring started a long association with the guy most of us called Whitey, who was also a rookie trying to break into the Major Leagues.*

Roberts's first day in training was his introduction to the real world of baseball.

He was trying to adapt his previous training in winter conditions up north to a warm climate in Florida. His leg muscles began to pull, and he had trouble adjusting to the soft sand common to Florida. Roberts remembered, "One day that first spring while I was still struggling with muscle pulls, I happened to be walking behind owner Bob Carpenter, unbeknownst to him. I overheard him say, 'Looks like I blew another $25,000.' Of course, that was the amount of my bonus, and I knew that he was talking about me. I had not yet pitched, and Bob's comment was upsetting, particularly because I thought I was there to pitch, not run."

Within a week, Roberts had his chance to prove his worth to the team and especially to Bob Carpenter. Robin Roberts threw his first pitch in an exhibition game against the Cardinals' B team. "In three innings I got nine consecutive outs, struck out four, and hit a triple. Of course, that was the first time I pitched for the Phillies and afterward everybody was very excited about my outing and nobody was worried about my legs anymore. I was sitting in the clubhouse after the game feeling very good about my performance." By the end of spring training he was transferred to the Wilmington Blue Rocks to sharpen his skills further.

However, by midsummer he was called up to pitch for the Philles. He was able to throw his first pitch against the Pittsburgh Pirates on June 18, 1948. The following spring he returned for training as a member of the Philadelphia Philles.

Throughout the Phillies' history there have been some very strict managers who demanded total obedience from their players. In some cases the players rebelled, but in most cases it was the manager who had the last word. However, in one specific case a manager had lost control of his players. In 1948 Eddie Sawyer became the manager of the Philadelphia Phillies. For years there had been a no-wife rule in Clearwater during spring training. Sawyer did not enforce the rule during the spring of 1950, "and since the Phils went on to win the pennant, he held a light rein in 1951. That was a mistake."

Robin Roberts in his memoirs commented on Sawyer's handling of the players and his overall attitude as a manager:

> *Eddie had a very hands-off leadership style that I did not grow to appreciate* [until] *much later in my baseball career. We knew who was boss, but he did not flaunt his authority or force himself on us. We had very few meetings, and Eddie had very few conversations with individual players. When he did talk to a player it was in private and had a purpose, usually to correct a mistake or give a quiet confidence boost. I personally did not have any kind of conversation with Eddie for almost a year after he became the Phillies' manager, except to say hello and goodbye each day. He never talked to me before I pitched. Most of the time I would read in the paper that I was starting so I would get a ball, warm up, and pitch the game. Sometimes I would hear from a coach that I was pitching, but I never heard from Eddie.*

The players upon their return for spring training in 1951 had arrived with a totally different attitude than that of Sawyer's. The players viewed training as beneath them and found every reason to avoid showing up at the field. A few would call in sick in order to go out fishing with their teammates. Sawyer's control of the team seemed to pour through his hands like sand. With the start of the season the Phillies weren't able to hold their title and dropped out of First Division. The following spring, Sawyer reintroduced his no-car, no-family rule into effect as the players returned for spring training. Orodenker stated in *The Phillies Reader* that

> *A couple of the boys, with fine, legal minds, installed their wives in rented homes and insisted that Clearwater was their legal residence. It was only*

after Sawyer threatened to move the training quarters that they sent their wives home. Another player rented a cottage for his wife outside of town, while he himself lived at the hotel with the team. Sawyer told him to stay away from the park until she went home. By this time, the discipline was too much and too late. The resentment against Sawyer was so great that his authority was gone.

Within a few short months Sawyer's admittance that he had lost control of his team forced Bob Carpenter to replace him with Steve O'Neill.

As the years passed, it was obvious a more modern park was needed, and one who strongly believed that was Jack Russell, a former Major League pitcher. Russell, a tall, handsome right-hander from Paris, Texas, had settled in Clearwater during his fifteen-year big league career with six clubs, had become involved in city affairs and elected to the city commission. At the 1954 Orange Bowl game in Miami, Russell met a Nashville architect whose firm specialized in ballparks and mentioned Clearwater's interest in a new park. He also mentioned the city had no money. After returning to Clearwater, Russell contacted the acquaintance from the Nashville firm of Marr and Holliman and talked him into sending him plans for a ballpark without charge. The firm had been involved in the building of similar parks in Miami and Tampa, the latter then under construction.

Russell waited a while before showing the plans to city officials, recalling, "I spent a lot of sleepless nights." When he finally did, the reaction was favorable. Soon thereafter, Mayor Herbert M. Brown announced, "It is apparent that the new municipal baseball park is a reality." The cost was to be financed by a $400,000 recreation revenue certificate issue. It was to have a cantilever roof with 4,744 seats and room for bleachers along the left field line, as well as a press box and broadcast booths.

Final city approval was given on May 10, and on June 21 a contract for $317,656 was awarded to the Clearwater Construction Company to build the park a hundred yards east of the old park. It was next to Green Field, used for football and baseball and situated between the Clearwater Athletic Field and the site of the new stadium. A new road was to separate the stadium and parking lot. Construction went smoothly and the stadium was dedicated on March 10, 1955, the day the Phillies opened their exhibition season. A crowd of 4,209 saw the Phillies beat the Detroit Tigers, 4–2, on a two-run double by third baseman Willie Jones.

Commissioner Ford Frick; league presidents Warren Giles and Will Harridge; Mayor Brown; City Manager Francis Middleton; the four city commissioners, including Russell; and the city's recreation board, headed by Eddie Moore, were among the notables at the dedication. Russell was given the job of introducing the baseball notables. In introducing Russell, the mayor made the surprise announcement that the park was to be named Jack Russell Stadium in tribute to his activities in promoting the growth of Clearwater, then a city of over forty thousand.

During the 1950s and 1960s, the civil rights movement began to make headway in destroying the Jim Crow laws of the old American South. However, for most African Americans, the changes came slowly in the century since the War Between the States. Even the Phillies were resistant in allowing African Americans to join their organization since Jackie Robinson had signed with the Dodgers in 1947. One account resides in Rich Westcott's *Tales from the Phillies Dugout*:

> *None gave the Major League's first African-American player in the 20th century more grief than the Phillies. Led by Tennessee-born manager Ben Chapman, the Phillies had razzed Robinson well beyond the limits of civility in the club's first meeting of the season with the Brooklyn Dodgers at Ebbets Field. A black cat was released, and racist taunts from the Phillies' dugout were indicative of the extreme bigotry of the Philadelphia team.*

This was one of many injustices the Phillies handed out to Jackie Robinson and his fellow teammates during his first season. It took a long while for the Phillies to learn the results of their bigotry; in fact, the ball club was the last of the National League teams to sign on an African American player.

In 1957 John Kennedy, a shortstop from the Kansas City Monarchs, made his debut with the Philadelphia Phillies during spring training in Clearwater. Kennedy was not the first African American to be signed by the Phillies; Teddy Washington was signed on in 1952 and two more black players were signed on as well. However, John Kennedy was signed on and was the first African American to make the squad, heading north from spring training in Clearwater. Sports columnist Claude Harrison wrote the following observation on John Kennedy in his column for the *Philadelphia Tribune*:

> *Bill Yancey, the Phillies baseball scout who came up with John Kennedy, is more than pleased with the reports coming out of Clearwater, Fla., the Phils' spring training base, about young Kennedy. Bill never talks too much about Kennedy's future, because as he puts it, "all I know is what I read in the papers." But on the other hand he did have something to say about Eddie Logan, the former Ridley Township High football and track star,*

> *who topped all of the Phillies' farm hands with a .384 average at Class D level in 1956. Logan, along with Kennedy, was given the once over at the Phillies' rookie training school during March. However, the school teachers sent Logan back to the minors and as you know held Kennedy over to train with the parent club...What we would like to know is what does he have to do in order to prove he's Major League material. At the beginning of the season word came out of Clearwater that he couldn't field. Yet he has made only one blunder. While on the other hand the player they paid $75,000 for makes two in one day. John's batting of .333 is second highest for the club. What more can the Phils ask?*

Kennedy played a total of five games before being sent back down, never to be heard of again. However, Chico Fernandez became the first black regular with the Phillies when he came to the team in a trade with the Dodgers late in spring training in 1957. As more African Americans were signed with the Phillies and its affiliates, boarding them was a problem during spring training in the South during the early to mid-1960s. While the white players stayed together at the hotel in Clearwater, the black players were barred from staying with their white counterparts in hotels. With the assistance of local black community leaders, the players were able to stay in the homes of African American families. From the late 1960s on, both white and black players were able to stay together in the hotels throughout Florida and the American South.

Bob Uecker, the master of one-liners who played for the Phillies in 1966 and 1967, once exclaimed on the subject of the Phillies' practice site at their Clearwater spring training base: "It's like playing on Iwo Jima!" Construction and completion in 1967 of the four-diamond Carpenter Complex, a joint venture of the Phillies and the city four miles east of Jack Russell Stadium, assured that the Phillies would be in Clearwater for years to come.

Over the decades, many Phillies trained at Jack Russell Stadium, whether as rookies or experienced players. Some were to become Hall of Famers, such as Robin Roberts, Tug McGraw and Mike Schmidt. Schmidt recounted how his first time training in Clearwater as a Philadelphia Phillies player was nearly a no-show. In 1976

> *the owners had locked the players out of camps as the continuing struggle over the basic terms of the eight-year-old Collective Bargaining Agreement* [CBA] *between the players and the owners began to get nasty. There was a lot of tension and anger and confusion in the air. Then, shortly after the seventeen-day lockout ended and the camps were opened on March 17.*

At the beginning of the 1980 season, most people felt things were going to be the same as previous years for the Philadelphia Phillies. In the words of Rich Wescott,

> *After a lackluster spring training, the 1980 Phillies got off to a mediocre start. Then they climbed atop the East Division standings for two days in May. Soon afterward, number-three starter Larry Christenson was lost for the season following elbow surgery, and the team began to drift downward. It briefly captured a half-game lead in mid-July, but by then Tug McGraw was on the sidelines with tendonitis. The Phils quickly fell out of the lead.*

However, within a few short games, the Phillies were able to regroup and entered into the fray with new energy. Eventually, the team made it into the playoffs. The Phillies beat the Kansas City Royals after the sixth game at Veterans Stadium in Philadelphia. This was the Phillies' first win in the World Series after their ninety-seven-year history as a team.

Every baseball team had a few men who were a unifying and driving force propelling the players to success. Paul Owens was one such man. In 1985 Paul "The Pope" Owens celebrated thirty years with the Phillies. The following biography was printed in the Clearwater Phillies inaugural season program:

> *Paul Owens, commonly referred today as the "The Pope," has been with the Phillies organization for thirty years. Owens began managing with the Phillies in Olean, New York, a Phillies minor league franchise. From Olean, Owens went on to scout for the Phillies organization. Moving up the organizational ladder, Owens later became the director of the Phillies minor league system. In 1972, Owens was named general manager of the Phillies. Taking the managerial spot on an interim basis for a brief period in 1972, Owens returned to the front office and transformed the Phillies into divisional winners in 1976. He has since guided the Phillies into the winningest record in the National League, both in total victories and in post season participation. In 1980, the Phillies that Owens assembled came through with the World Championship. "The Pope" continued as general manager until 1983, when he was called upon to return as field manager of the Phillies. Owens's return sparked the club, with the Phillies defeating the Los Angeles Dodgers in the National League Playoffs. Owens will now return to the Phillies front office as top player advisor. Whatever the role, Paul Owens has proven to be at the top of his profession in every capacity. The Phillies salute you, Paul Owens!*

During the 1980s Ron Timpanaro served as the field supervisor and was responsible for the upkeep of the playing field as well as the overall facilities in and around the stadium. Jack Russell Stadium had been named the Baseball Diamond of the Year for 1988. The award—sponsored by Beam Clay, the Sports Turf Managers Association and *Sports Turf* magazine—is a recognition of excellence and professionalism in maintaining outstanding, safe, professional-quality baseball diamonds. Entries were judged in three categories: Professional Diamonds, College Diamonds and School, Municipal or Park Diamonds. The field at Jack Russell Stadium won in the Professional Diamond category. It was selected winner out of over forty baseball fields on both the Major League and minor league levels. The nonstop effort put forth by Ron Timpanaro and his staff of Opie and Ron Cheek contributed to the excellent environment at the stadium.

Rich Wescott, renowned baseball historian, recounted how some ballplayers would pass their time while on the road for exhibition games during spring training in the late 1980s and early 1990s. Taking on a scene out of *Field of Dreams* came this lighthearted account:

> *There's nothing duller for baseball players than a long bus ride in spring training. Sometimes, however, a little comedy can liven up the trip. The Phillies were on their way back to Clearwater after an exhibition game, and some of the fun lovers were in the back of the bus partaking of a few beverages. Darren Daulton (1983, 1985–97) had just signed a contract of substantial proportions, and some of his busmates were discussing the catcher's good fortune.*
>
> *"You know what you need to do, Dutch?" John Kruk said. "You need to build a big mansion, and we'll all live in it, party, have a good time, and play ball."*
>
> *From another seat in the back of the bus came the voice of Pete Incaviglia: "If you build it," he said, "we will come."*

Apart from spring training in Clearwater, baseball was big business in the Tampa Bay region, and there had been a drive to secure a National League franchise for the area for decades. A few sites were considered in Pinellas County, including Clearwater, for a future site for a stadium to be constructed if a baseball franchise was awarded to the Tampa Bay area. Eventually, St. Petersburg was chosen to become home of Tropicana Field. In 1989 the Florida Suncoast Dome opened and the lobbying for a team commenced. In the meantime the stadium served as the temporary home of the NHL Tampa Bay Lightning as well as a site for Arena Football League and basketball games. On March 9, 1995, Major League Baseball awarded St. Petersburg the expansion franchise and the Tampa Bay Devil Rays were born. They began playing during the 1998 inaugural season.

After well over fifty years, the facilities at Jack Russell Stadium began to be antiquated and maintenance began to be costly. The Phillies and the City of Clearwater began to negotiate for new facilities. The plan was to relocate the stadium near the Carpenter Complex near U.S. Highway 19, combining all of the Phillies facilities into one location. In addition, the new location would give the Phillies the opportunity to grow. The last spring training season in Jack Russell Stadium was in 2003.

In 1947 the Philadelphia Phillies arrived in Clearwater to begin their spring training at old Green Field. Seen here are members of the Phillies at the Clearwater Railroad Depot waiting to be transported to their lodgings. The photograph was taken in 1949. *From the Collection of AdeQ Historical Archives.*

Phillies hustling about in the Clearwater Athletic Field during the 1950 spring training season. Following their training, the Phillies obtained the 1950 pennant. *From the Collection of AdeQ Historical Archives.*

Ritchie Ashburn at batting practice during the 1947 spring training season. The following year Ashburn was named the *Sporting News* Rookie of the Year. The future Hall of Famer would lead the National League in hits three times and in batting average three times in the 1950s. In addition he served as the Phillies broadcaster from 1971 until his death in 1997. *From the Collection of AdeQ Historical Archives.*

Ford Frick (left), president of the National League, and Eddie Sawyer (right), manager of the Philadelphia Phillies, lend an ear while umpire Bill Stewart discusses some of the new baseball rule changes at the Phillies spring camp in Clearwater in a photograph dated March 1, 1950. The league sent umpires to each of the spring training camps to clarify the rules' changes. *From the Collection of AdeQ Historical Archives.*

Jack Russell Stadium opened in 1955. During construction spring training games were held in the aged Green Field facility located adjacent to the construction site. Upon the opening of the new stadium, the old field was razed and the site became a parking lot for spectators. *From the Collection of AdeQ Historical Archives.*

Another view of Jack Russell Stadium during the early 1960s. The stadium also served as a home for the Clearwater Bombers, one of Clearwater's oldest softball teams. *From the Collection of AdeQ Historical Archives.*

Andy Seminick, one of the steadiest catchers to ever wear a Phillies uniform, is seen photographed at Jack Russell Stadium in the mid-1950s. Overall, he played fifteen years in the Majors and had few equals as a handler of pitchers and as a guardian of the plate. He was best known for being a solid veteran of the "Whiz Kids." In 1950, when the Phillies won the pennant, he had his finest season, hitting .288 with 24 home runs. Upon his retirement as a player in 1956, Seminick managed the Phillies Farm System for eight years, rejoined the Phillies as a coach in 1967 and served with them for three years. He later returned to the minors to manage for three more years. In 1962 Seminick became the first coach for the Florida Institute of Technology Panthers Baseball Team and assisted in setting up the sports program for the university. In 1973 he became a scout. On March 8, 1987, the former Phillies player was honored by the Florida Institute of Technology with "Andy Seminick Day," and the university's baseball team played against the Philadelphia Phillies. *From the Collection of AdeQ Historical Archives.*

Eddie Sawyer served as the Phillies manager from 1948 to 1952 and from 1958 to 1960. His management of the team was controversial and led to his dismissal by Carpenter in 1952. He later served as a scout for the Philadelphia Phillies and Kansas City Royals in the 1960s and 1970s. *From the Collection of AdeQ Historical Archives.*

Alvin Dark during the 1960 spring training season in Clearwater. *From the Collection of AdeQ Historical Archives.*

Tony Gonzalez at bat during spring training in the early 1960s. After being traded by General Manager John Quinn in 1960, Gonzalez served a productive nine years with the Phillies. During his career he got 1,485 hits and his lifetime average was .286. *From the Collection of AdeQ Historical Archives.*

Bobby Wine at the newly constructed Carpenter Field. In the distance is U.S. Highway 19. Wine played for the Phillies from 1960 to 1968. Carpenter Field was built in 1967 as an additional training facility. *From the Collection of AdeQ Historical Archives.*

Ruben Amaro played for the Philadelphia Phillies from 1960 to 1965. In later years he served as a scout for the Phillies and discovered top-notch players from Latin America such as Julio Franco, Al Sanchez and Juan Samuel. *From the Collection of AdeQ Historical Archives.*

During the 1970s the Philadelphia Phillies made the Quality Inn/Sandcastle Hotel their winter home. It was located downtown, overlooking Clearwater Bay on Osceola Avenue and Drew Street. The hotel boasted "more than one hundred spacious, well-appointed rooms [that] provide ideal resort accommodations for a fun weekend or a vacation." The Harborside Restaurant offered a "varied selection of shellfish and succulent Bouillabaisse," as well as Southern fried chicken and grilled steaks. Members of the Phillies definitely spent their time in Harry's New York Bar, which offered dancing and entertainment. *From the Collection of AdeQ Historical Archives.*

Greg Luzinski at bat during spring training at Carpenter Field during the 1970s. He played for the Philadelphia Phillies from 1970 to 1980. Carpenter Field was a four-field complex that was established in 1967 by Paul Owens. After Owens's death, the complex was renamed the Paul Owens Training Facility in 2004. *From the Collection of AdeQ Historical Archives.*

Another view of Jack Russell Stadium as seen from the outfield. *From the Collection of AdeQ Historical Archives.*

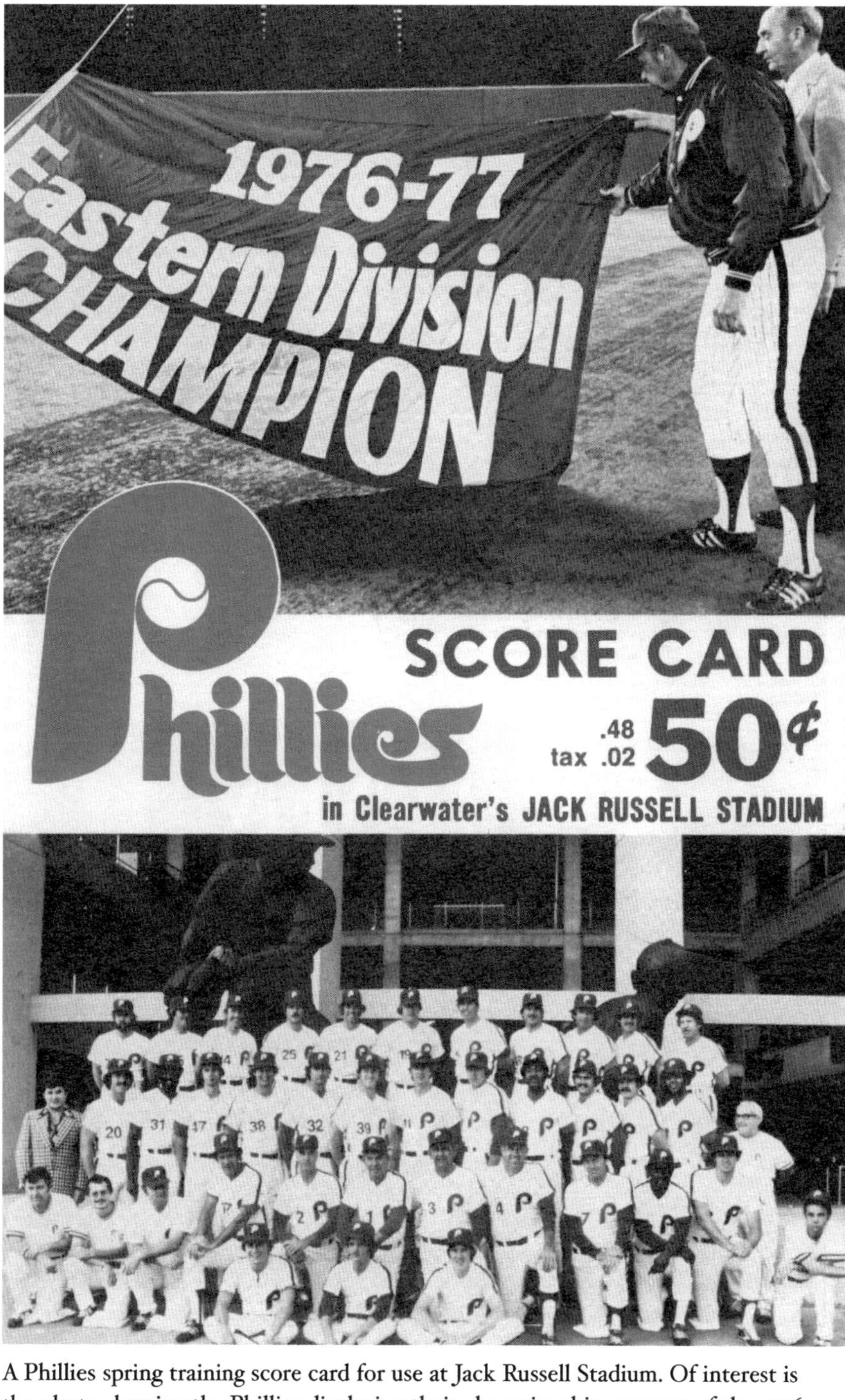

A Phillies spring training score card for use at Jack Russell Stadium. Of interest is the photo showing the Phillies displaying their championship pennant of the 1976–77 Eastern Division. *From the Collection of AdeQ Historical Archives.*

A team photograph of the Philadelphia Phillies at Jack Russell Stadium in 1984. Mike Schmidt (first row, far right) and Tug McGraw (third row, fourth from left) are among the players in this photograph. Manager Paul Owens, with jersey number 5, is seated in the front row between coaches John Felske and Deron Johnson. *From the Collection of AdeQ Historical Archives.*

Jack Russell Stadium was named the Baseball Diamond of the Year for 1988 by the Sports Turf Managers Association with Beam Clay and *Sports Turf* magazine. Pictured are Ron Timpanaro and his staff of Opie and Ron Cheek. The composite photograph was from the 1989 Phillies Spring Training Program. *Courtesy of the Philadelphia Phillies and from the Collection of AdeQ Historical Archives.*

A classic image from the cover of the 1989 Philadelphia Phillies Spring Training Program showing Jack Russell Stadium. *Courtesy of the Philadelphia Phillies and from the Collection of AdeQ Historical Archives.*

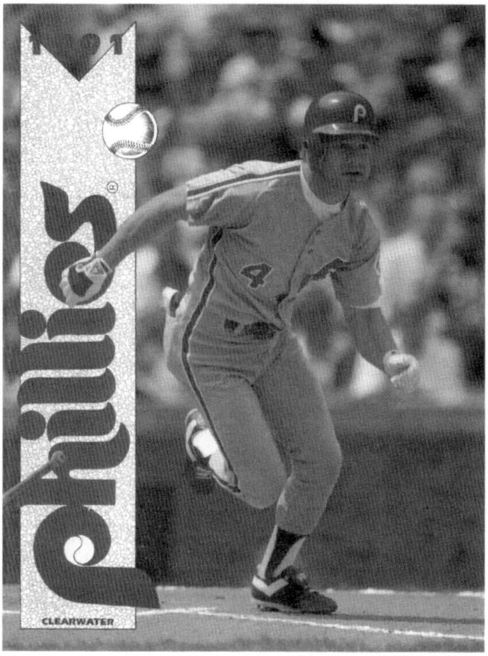

This 1991 Spring Training Program shows Phillies outfielder Lenny Dykstra on the cover. Dykstra played for the Philadelphia Phillies from 1989 to 1996. *Courtesy of the Philadelphia Phillies and from the Collection of AdeQ Historical Archives.*

The Phillies introduced their new mascot, Philly Phanatic, and made special appearances at Jack Russell Stadium during spring training and even some of the Clearwater Phillies home games. *Courtesy Philadelphia Phillies and from the Collection of AdeQ Historical Archives.*

A Philadelphia Phillies Spring Training Program from 1998. Among those pictured on the cover are some of the best-known Phillies players of the 1990s, such as Curt Schilling, Garrett Stephenson, Scott Rolen, Mike Lieberthal, Ricky Bottalico and Rico Brogan. The issue also remembered the passing of Ritchie Ashburn, who had died in 1997. Ashburn was named to the Hall of Fame in 1995. *Courtesy Philadelphia Phillies and from the Collection of AdeQ Historical Archives.*

Jack Russell Stadium as it appeared in 2006. Three years after the Phillies moved to their new facilities at Bright House Networks Field, the only vestige of the Phillies presence there was the souvenir shack still bearing the faded logo of the team and street signs that still designated 800 Phillies Drive. *Photo by the author.*

A Lasting Legacy
The Phillies' Minor League Teams

The Florida State League originated as a Class D league in 1919 with teams in Bartow, Bradenton, Lakeland, Orlando, Sanford and Tampa. It was during this period that a relocated Florida state franchise team called the Daytona Beach Islanders arrived in Clearwater in 1924 and renamed themselves the Clearwater Pelicans—they only lasted for one season. The league fluctuated between four and eight teams for eight years until closing down in 1928. The league resumed play in 1936 and has continued uninterrupted, except for a four-year (1942–45) suspension during World War II. It remained a Class D league until 1963, when it was changed to a Class A status. Many players from the Florida State League have gone on to the Hall of Fame, including Stan Musial, Early Wynn, Al Lopez, Johnny Bench, Jim Palmer, Rod Carew, Ferguson Jenkins and Rollie Fingers. In all, twelve hundred players from the Florida State League have spent time in the American and National Leagues.

Before 2002, the league was classified as a High A league, indicating its status as a Class A league with the highest level of competition within its classification, and the fifth step between rookie ball and the Major Leagues. Although Minor League Baseball, the umbrella organization for minor leagues that are affiliated with Major League Baseball, has eliminated the distinction between High A and other full-season A leagues, most Major

League teams still use this league as a standard promotion step. A few draftees, generally early round draftees with college experience, will be assigned to a High A team upon signing a professional contract, but most High A players do not reach that level until their third or fourth year of professional play. Currently, the league is divided into an East Division and a West Division. The twelve-member teams play a 140 game schedule with 70 games at home and 70 games on the road. The six-team East Division and six-team West Division play a split season with the first half ending in June and the second half ending in September.

Four teams participate in the playoffs. Winners of both halves within each division play each other in a best-of-three series for the division championships. If there is a repeat division winner, a wild-card team qualifies for the playoffs. The division champions move on to the league championship series and play a best-of-five series. The Gainesville G-Men were once a part of this league when it restarted in 1936. They continued until they hit financial difficulties in 1952.

The Watson Spoelstra Florida State League Championship Trophy is presented each year to the winning team of the season-ending playoff series. It was initiated in 1979 and travels among the winning teams. The trophy is named after Watson Spoelstra, a Detroit sportswriter who approached Baseball Commissioner Bowie Kuhn in 1973 with the idea of organizing a program to provide weekly chapel services for every Major League team. Kuhn granted approval and Baseball Chapel was created as a nonprofit organization. To this day, chapel services are held for teams in the Majors, minors and independent leagues during the regular season, playoffs and the World Series.

In 1985 the Clearwater Phillies came into existence with Ramon Aviles as manager. Aviles was a former player in the Phillies, Red Sox and Rangers organizations. A native of Puerto Rico, he attended a regional college in Arecibo, Puerto Rico. Aviles was signed by the Red Sox scout Pedro Vazquez as a free agent on November 7, 1969. He began his career with the Red Sox at Greenville in the Western Carolina League. While still with the Red Sox, Ramon led the International League shortstops in fielding percentage (.952) in 1977. The following year, the Phillies obtained the rights to Aviles. He appeared in 27 games in 1980. After briefly playing for the Rangers in 1981, Aviles returned to the Phillies to make several playoff appearances. In 1982 Ramon spent the entire year in the big leagues. Aviles made his managerial debut in the Northwest League in 1984. He led his team to a 38–36 record and a second-place finish. The Clearwater Phillies statistics for 1985 were 69–72 (.489) and they finished fourth in the Florida State League Western Division. Ramon

Aviles served only one season as manager and was followed by Ron Clark as the manager for the 1986 season.

Jack Russell Stadium served as the site for the Twenty-seventh Florida State League All-Star Game on June 25, 1988. Glenn Gulliver became manager of the Clearwater Phillies in 1989. Gulliver, a former infielder, spent ten years (1976–85) in the Baltimore organization and never played below the Double A level. He saw Major League action twice with the Orioles in 1982 (.200 in fifty games) and in 1983 (.231 in 23 games). He had his best season in 1983 with Rochester, batting .309 with 11 home runs, 63 RBIs and 117 walks. He managed in the Orioles farm system for three years (1986 and 1988 at Bluefield, and 1987 at Hagerstown, taking that club to the playoffs). He was replaced by Lee Elia the following season.

The Clearwater Phillies made it to the playoffs for the Florida State League Championships in 1991, 1992 and 1993. Andy Carter threw a nine-inning no-hitter at Jack Russell Stadium on August 23, 1992, as part of the only double no-hitter in minor league history. That game ended in a 1–0 victory for the Clearwater Phillies over the Winter Haven Red Sox. The following season, the Clearwater Phillies reached the playoffs, where Clearwater defeated Charlotte two games to one. The Phillies later defeated the St. Lucie Mets three games to one, winning the 1993 Florida State League Championship. The Phillies made it to the playoffs again in 1996 and 1999.

The Clearwater Phillies adopted a new mascot for the team. Phil E. Phox made his debut in April 1996 and became the face of the Clearwater Phillies. A team sports card of the day described the mascot in the following manner: "He can be found mingling with fans at games or representing the Phillies around town. One thing is certain, he loves attention and Phillies baseball. According to Phil, the Phillie Phanatic is his best friend." The oversized fox dressed in a Phillies jersey and Clearwater cap was popular among fans, especially children, and replaced another mascot, Philbert, who was adopted in the years between 1985 and 1995. Phil E. Phox was discontinued after the 2003 season.

In 1999 another minor league team affiliated with the Philadelphia Phillies was formed in Clearwater. The rookie-class Gulf Coast Phillies formed within the Gulf Coast League. This league operates in Florida and is a rookie league with a season running from mid-June to late August. Teams within the Gulf Coast League generally play in the minor league spring training complexes of their parent Major League clubs and are uniformly owned by those parent clubs. Their games are usually played for very few spectators and are usually played in the afternoon. The games of the Gulf Coast League are the least competitive of all the minor league games, as most of the players have just been drafted in that year's entry draft and are there to develop skills under their employer's tutelage rather than to win games or entertain fans. To differentiate between teams of the Gulf Coast League and the Florida State League, the Gulf Coast teams are not referred to by their home city, but simply by their parent club's name and the prefix "GCL" or "Gulf Coast." Some of these teams share stadiums with their club's High A affiliate in the Florida State League, which can lead to confusion. Florida State teams use the city name—such as the Clearwater Threshers, three levels above the Gulf Coast Phillies.

During the month of June 2002, Roly DeArmas was getting ready for his second season as manager of the Gulf Coast Phillies when he found out he had a new assignment: instead of coaching the short-season Gulf Coast League team, he would be taking over the advanced Class A team in Clearwater. The parent club had demoted John Morris, a former Cardinals outfielder who played in the 1987 World Series.

John Morris, in his first year as a manager in the Phillies organization, was assigned to be a hitting coach with the Gulf Coast Phillies. Clearwater ended the first half of its season with ten straight losses and was a league-worst 22–50, twenty-one games behind the first-place Tampa Yankees. Before changing managers, the Phillies made numerous player moves and shored up their defense by signing two minor league veterans, right fielder Troy McNaughton and first baseman Troy Farnsworth, to support Clearwater's demoralized pitching staff. "Their record concerns me, and I've tried to piece together a lineup to improve the club because we're trying to create a positive attitude for our young pitchers there," Phillies farm director Mike Arbuckle said to *Baseball America*.

DeArmas had been a part of the Phillies organization for twenty-three years (1973–93 and 2001–02) as a player and coach. He spent the winter working at baseball academies in Venezuela and the Dominican Republic. "These are just some of the things that happen in baseball," said DeArmas, who was the Clearwater manager in 1987. "I'm a Phillie at heart and I always want to help the organization, but this is a tough situation. John [Morris] is a friend and I know it's got to be hard on his family."

DeArmas met with the players after taking the position but did not make drastic changes. "I didn't know much about the players before coming here," DeArmas said. "They're all good kids who have kept their heads up so far. I'm just going to keep stressing the fundamentals and do some extra work with them. Other than that, we'll just keep on trucking and whatever happens, happens."

At the same time, Clearwater third baseman Juan Richardson had been on a tear since being named Most Valuable Player of the Florida State

League All-Star Game in the latter half of June 2002. Richardson hit two home runs in an inning, including a grand slam. He was the first Clearwater player to hit two home runs in an inning and the first in the Florida State League during the 2004 season.

Among much fanfare the Clearwater Phillies changed their name to the Clearwater Threshers after their move to Bright House Networks Field from Jack Russell Stadium in 2004. Hall of Famer Mike Schmidt recounted how he became the new manager of the Threshers:

> *I recieved a call in the fall of 2003 from Ed Wade saying that the Clearwater job was available: Would I be interested? He touched softly on some of the requirements and gave me a few days to think it over…Donna* [my wife] *convinced me that I needed to work every day and to keep my mind active…So Donna and I put together a plan to exist on a far different schedule than we were used to for the next seven months. Then I went to Clearwater to interview with Ed Wade and the Phillies' minor league director, Mike Arbuckle, where I got a more detailed explanation of what the job entailed. Mike outlined minor league organizational policies and schedules, emphasized some "horror" stories from past years, and generally painted a very clear picture that this was in no way, shape, or form a glamorous job. Oh, and the pay wasn't very good. There wasn't really anything about the job that should have been of interest to me, except the challenge it presented. The interview went well, and I was offered the position. I was to become the first Hall of Famer ever to manage in the minor leagues.*

Schmidt's roster for the 2004 Clearwater Threshers consisted of a mixture of white, black and Latino players, as well as the following experienced coaches: Steve Schrenk (pitching coach), Manny Amador (hitting and third base coach) and Dan Roberts (first base coach). Of interest is the fact that Dan Roberts is the son of Phillies Hall of Famer Robin Roberts. From 1986 to 2000, Roberts was the head baseball coach for the United States Military Academy in West Point, where he was the all-time wins leader. He was named the Patriot League Coach of the Year in 1995 and 1997. He coached for the Clearwater Threshers for the 2004 and 2005 seasons.

The season was cut short because of a series of hurricanes that hit Florida during the latter part of the summer. Schmidt commented that "the season ended with a storm—make that two storms, Charley and Frances. On August 14, Hurricane Charley made landfall in Boca Grande, 150 miles south of our stadium. It shut the league down for several days, and caused Sarasota and Fort Myers to alter their schedules. Our stadium became a hurricane shelter. Once we resumed play, we got about two weeks in before Frances came along. Season over."

After serving as manager of the Clearwater Threshers for a season, Mike Schmidt decided to move on to other ventures. Greg Legg became the next Threshers manager for the 2005 and 2006 baseball seasons. He had joined the Phillies family when he was drafted by the Phillies in 1982. His playing career was highlighted in 1986 when he made his Major League debut where he hit .459 (9–20) in eleven games for the Phillies. His career spanned into 1994 when he was summoned to active duty for the Scranton/Wilkes-Barre Red Barons on April 29 while coaching in Clearwater. His coaching career officially began in 1995 as a coach for the Clearwater Phillies. Greg spent the next season as a coach with Scranton before his managerial career began. In addition, Ken Dominguez and Scott Lovecamp came in as the new coaches for the 2005 season.

Ken Dominguez began his first season as a Phillies coach after spending time with the Chicago White Sox and New York Yankees organizations. During the 2004 season Ken managed the Winston-Salem Warthogs of the Single A Carolina League. Overall, Ken owns a 263–249 managerial record over eight minor league seasons. He earned Manager of the Year honors in the Gulf Coast League in 1996 after guiding Tampa to the Gulf Coast League Championship.

After spending eight seasons as a pitching coach in the Pirates organization and as a Pirates scout for Georgia and Florida between 1994 and 1996, Scott Lovecamp joined the Clearwater Threshers as the replacement for Manny Amador. He spent the previous two seasons as the Lynchburg Hillcats pitching coach. In addition, Lovecamp spent the 1999 and 2001 seasons as the pitching coach for the Pirates AA affiliate, the Altoona Curve. Since taking on the job, he has also served as a coach for children during the annual Clearwater Threshers Summer Baseball Camp and has been quite popular among his young pupils.

The 2006 season marked Legg's tenth season as a manager in the Phillies system. He had managed the following teams since 1997: Batavia Muckdogs (1997, 1999), Martinsville Phillies (1998), Piedmont Boll Weevils (2000), Lakewood Blue Claws (2001), Reading Phillies (2002–2004) and the Clearwater Threshers (since 2005). A couple of his accomplishments include the best record in minor league baseball in 2000 with a 90–47 (.657) mark. That season he was also named the South Atlantic League Manager of the Year. Overall, Legg has compiled a 515–540 career record and a 4–6 (.400) post-season mark in nine managerial seasons.

Greg Legg's coaches for the 2005 season were Dan Roberts and Scott Lovecamp. Scott began working as the pitching coach for the Threshers in 2005. He previously spent eight seasons as a pitching coach in the Pittsburgh Pirates organization. Lovecamp performed his coaching duties with the Lynchburg Hillcats in 2003 and 2004. He spent the 1999 and 2001 seasons with the Altoona Curve of the Eastern League.

John Timberlake, director of Florida operations and general manager of the Clearwater Threshers, was named the Executive of the Year by the Florida State League for 2005. In addition, Opie Cheek was honored with the Sportsturf Manager of the Year. Though the Threshers were last in the composite standing of clubs of the 2005 season, the team did make some worthwhile achievements: Jake Blalock was batting leader for 134 games; and Zach Segovia was pitching leader for 14 games lost, 98 runs allowed, 89 earned runs allowed, 18 home runs allowed and 17 hit batters.

After two seasons, the Clearwater Threshers introduced their new mascot, Phinley the Shark, during the first home game at Bright House Networks Field on April 6, 2006. The birth of the Threshers mascot is vividly described in the team's official website. The account is as follows:

> *On a beautiful January day, John Timberlake, Dan McDonough, Jason Adams and Opie Cheek chartered a fishing boat. They had planned a day of relaxation before a new season of Threshers Baseball. The guys were especially excited because of the number of sharks rumored to inhabit the Gulf of Mexico during the winter. John, Dan and Jason cast their lines while Opie tried to explain the difference between St. Augustine and Bermuda grass to the captain.*
>
> *After an hour without so much as a nibble on their bait, the guys decided it was time to eat. Luckily they had stocked up a supply of Philly cheese steaks from LaSpada's for the trip. Just as Jason bit into his sandwich, the boat violently lurched. The abrupt movement knocked him off-balance and sent his cheese steak over board. A moment later, John felt a tug on his line. Immediately he was in a life and death struggle to reel in an unknown monster of the deep. Dan and Jason were amazed with John's fishing prowess. Without even breaking a sweat, John hauled up the largest shark any of them had ever seen, with the Philly cheese steak still in his powerful jaws.*
>
> *Opie and the captain even stopped talking about Kentucky Blue Grass in awe of this spectacle. Dan devised an idea to chum the water with the rest of the Philly cheese steaks to lure the shark to shore. It worked! Once docked the captain took a closer look and they realized that they had caught a rare and elusive Thresher Landshark! Dan looked at the shark, imagined the possibilities and proclaimed, "Let's Make a Deal!" Within minutes an agreement was written and endorsed. The document named Phinley the shark as the Threshers #1 phan. Additionally, he received all*

the Philly cheese steaks he could eat and all the hugs he could handle from the Threshers faithful phans. In return, Phinley is the point-shark for the Threshers nation.

Greg Gross came in as the hitting coach for the Clearwater Threshers at the start of the 2006 season. His first season with the Threshers was his second season as a minor league hitting coach. Gross was the Phillies hitting coach from 2002 to 2004 before he joined Batavia for the 2005 season. The former outfielder spent seventeen seasons in the Major Leagues, of which ten were spent with the Phillies. He owns a .287 career batting average and he ranks fourth all-time with 143 pinch hits. In addition, Jason Kirkman came on as athletic trainer. Jason began his fourth season in the Phillies organization, where he spent the last two seasons as the athletic trainer for the Lakewood Blue Claws. Kirkman also served as an athletic trainer in the Western Baseball League and the Western Hockey League.

At times, injured players from the Phillies joined the Threshers during their rehabilitation. During the 2006 season Philadelphia Phillies pitcher Randy Wolf was added to the Clearwater Threshers roster for a rehab assignment. His next scheduled start was on Tuesday, June 13 at 7:05 p.m. at Bright House Networks Field versus the Fort Myers Miracle. The left-hander was recovering from "Tommy John" surgery performed in July 2005. The six-year Major Leaguer has tallied a 65–60 career record with a 4.14 ERA in 182 games. Initial plans were to have Wolf rejoin the Phillies rotation in July. The Phillies were at 32–27, which placed them second in the National League East at the time. The Phillies selected Wolf in the second round of the 1997 draft from Pepperdine University, where he garnered All-Conference honors in three straight years.

As most players move up and down the minor league ladder, others seem to have the gift of rising up the ladder until they reach the Major League. Phillies future center fielder Greg Golson was promoted to Clearwater. He was added to the roster during the Threshers' 2006 season and saw his first action in a game against Brevard County. Golson, age twenty, stands six feet tall and weighs 190 pounds. He bats and throws from the right side. He was drafted in the first round (twenty-first overall) of the June 2004 draft out of John B. Connally High School in Austin, Texas. Since signing with the Phillies, Golson spent time with the Gulf Coast League Phillies (R) and the Lakewood Blueclaws (A). In 2004 he led the Gulf Coast Phillies with a .295 batting average, 34 runs, 8 triples and 12 stolen bases in 47 games. Following the Gulf Coast League season, he spent some time in the Florida Instructional League and then was promoted to Lakewood in 2005. He led the Blueclaws in stolen bases during the

2005 season with 25 and was leading in stolen bases again in 2006 with 23 before his promotion to Clearwater. Golson also saw limited action with the big league club during spring training 2005 and 2006. Golson was named Phillies Minor League Player of the Month for June 2006 and he has been rated as the fourth best prospect in the Phillies minor league system by *Baseball America*. Another honor he achieved was the 2003 Aflac All-American High School Baseball Classic in San Diego. For him there is a light at the end of the tunnel.

Clearwater Threshers pitcher Julio De La Cruz threw a complete game no-hitter versus the Sarasota Reds at Bright House Networks Field in Clearwater on Friday night. It only took De La Cruz ninety-four pitches in the nine-inning gem that the Threshers won 5–0. He struck out five batters and limited the Reds to two base runners: one on a walk in the fourth and one on an error in the seventh. A crowd of 5,906 rose to their feet just before the game ended on a looping line drive to second baseman Tim Moss. Brian Burgamy starred offensively for the Threshers. He scored what proved to be the only necessary run in the first inning and added insurance with a three-run homer in the eighth. It was the first no-hitter thrown by a Threshers pitcher and only the second in Clearwater's history. Andy Carter threw the other at Jack Russell Stadium on August 23, 1992, as part of the only double no-hitter in minor league history. That game ended in a 1–0 victory for the Clearwater Phillies over the Winter Haven Red Sox.

Julio improved to 2–1 with a 2.63 ERA in four August starts. In 27.1 innings he struck out 14 batters while limiting opponents to a .182 batting average. Previously, he was named Phillies Minor League Pitcher of the Week (June 26–July 2, 2006) for his efforts. For the 2006 season, he stood at 6–9 with a 4.11 ERA in 25 games. The near perfect game capped off a successful Pitch for Pink promotion that raised thousands of dollars for breast cancer research and awareness. The win pulled the Threshers to a 1.5 game deficit behind the West Division, leading the Fort Myers Miracles.

In all there were quite a few records set by the Threshers during the 2006 season. Brandon Florence set the Clearwater record for hits in a season with 163, breaking Rusty McNamara's record of 154 set in 1998. Brian Burgamy set the record for runs scored in a season with 110, beating the previous record of 93 runs by Gary Burnham in 1998. Burgamy also tied the Clearwater record for walks in a season with 88. He was later promoted to Double A Reading with two weeks left in the season. The season for the Clearwater Threshers made great strides on and off the field. The team finished with a 67–72 record, which was the best during the Threshers' three years of existence. The Threshers battled to the end in the West Division pennant chase of the Florida State League, leading the division as late as August 13. The team posted a 24–12 home record in the second half of the season.

Over the years, the uniforms worn by the minor league team in Clearwater went through small changes up until 2004. Since the creation of the Clearwater Phillies in 1985, the team wore nearly the same uniforms as those worn by the Major League club. Basically, the jersey's Phillies logo were Swiss-stitched on a patch, then sewn on the front of the jersey. The numbers on the back and sleeve were two layers and two colors of tackle twill. The players' names on the back were sewn in tackle twill on a plate. Occasionally, commemorative patches were sewn onto the sleeves, such as the minor league hundred-year anniversary patch that was worn on the right sleeve during the 2001 season. The change of the team's name from the Clearwater Phillies to the Clearwater Threshers in 2004 brought in a new image and a drastic change in the design, concept and use of the team's uniforms.

The Threshers brought in a wide assortment of uniforms and caps to be used in their inaugural season. Minor league baseball has a three-year requirement for any new logo or team. There were three basic types of uniforms used by the team: home (cream), away (gray) and batting practice (blue). The home and away jerseys sport the team's name across the front and a palm tree on the sleeve, and an American flag is applied on the back along with the player's last name and number. The caps featured a shark about to catch a baseball. The blue batting practice uniform and red cap, sporting a slightly different logo of a shark with a baseball bat, can be worn at home only—though it has been observed to be worn on some away games, when the extreme Florida heat and humidity is at its climax. Carrie Jenkins noted in 2005 that "five hats correspond home, away, batting practice, Sunday and alternate…The starting pitcher determines the uniform top and hat." But what sets the Threshers apart from other minor league teams—and even the Major League teams—is the use of specially adapted jerseys for special events and charities. These jerseys range from red-white-and-blue jerseys worn on the Fourth of July during the 2005 season to jerseys in the style of Hawaiian shirts, with a unique logo of a parrot atop the team's name, that were worn on Tropical Paradise Night on June 28, 2006. Knowing how to market the team well and raise money for worthwhile charities, the Threshers even sell their special event–themed jerseys following the game; such was the case with the pink jerseys worn by the team for Breast Cancer Awareness Night on August 18, 2006. One can only look forward in the future to see what new and exciting styles the Threshers will bring out in their uniforms.

It had been announced at the end of the minor league season of 2006 that there was a shakeup within the Phillies affiliate system. The

Philadelphia Phillies announced a two-year working agreement with the Williamsport Crosscutters in the short-season Class A New York–Pennsylvania League, thereby leaving Batavia after nearly twenty years. Steve Noworyta, director of the Phillies' minor leagues, commented: "Relocating our short-season team to Williamsport continues our plan of getting as many of our league teams as close as possible to Philadelphia. With AAA moving to the Lehigh Valley in 2008, the lone exception will be Clearwater. The great facilities in Clearwater will continue to be home for the Threshers and the Gulf Coast Rookie League team."

Many of the players from the Clearwater Threshers eventually make it to the Major Leagues. Scott Mathieson, age twenty-two, was a former Clearwater Thresher promoted to the Phillies' Major League roster during the 2006 season. Mathieson pitched very well for the Reading Phillies (AA) all season long. His 2006 record with Reading was 6–2 with a 3.05 ERA. His six wins were the most for a Reading pitcher in 2006. He also led Reading in innings pitched (85.2) and strikeouts (95). Mathieson spent the entire 2005 season in Clearwater (A) and also made an appearance for the club in 2006 spring training. He participated in the 2005 Futures game during All-Star Weekend and was also a member of Team Canada for the 2005 World Cup and the 2006 World Baseball Classic. Mathieson, a six-foot-three, 190-pound right-handed pitcher, was the Phillies seventeenth round selection in the 2002 amateur June draft out of Aldergrove Secondary School in British Columbia, Canada.

In all, since the debut of the Clearwater Phillies, there have been no fewer than forty-six players who made it to the Majors. The following list of players have taken the field for the Phillies' minor league affiliate in Clearwater. A majority played for the Clearwater Phillies (1985–2003), but the Threshers produced Major Leaguer Elizardo Ramirez (Phillies and Reds) in just two seasons of existence. The players are Marlon Anderson, Andy Ashby, Ezequiel Astacio, Kim Batiste, Gary Bennett, Ricky Bottalico, Jason Boyd, Eude Brito, Frank Brooks, Pat Burrell, Andy Carter, Dave Coggin, Pat Combs, Andy Dominique, Dave Doster, Brandon Duckworth, Adam Eaton, Bobby Estalella, Johnny Estrada, Tony Fiore, Gavin Floyd, Marvin Freeman, Geoff Geary, Wayne Gomes, Ryan Howard, Ron Jones, Ricky Jordan, Eric Junge, Jason Kershner, Mike Lieberthal, Anderson Machado, Ryan Madson, Jason Michaels, Mickey Morandini, Nick Punto, Elizardo Ramirez, Wally Richie, Scott Rolen, Jimmy Rollins, Bruce Ruffin, Carlos Silva, Kevin Stocker, Reggie Taylor, Robinson Tejeda, Chase Utley and Eric Valent. In the years to come, this Phillies affiliate will continue to generate players for the Major Leagues and continue the traditions of the game.

Donnie Elliot of the Clearwater Phillies on the pitching mound during the 1992 season. The Clearwater Phillies were formed in 1985 as a Class A minor league affiliate of the Philadelphia Phillies. Note the Phillies-style ball cap in use by the Clearwater team between 1985 and 1992. *Courtesy Philadelphia Phillies and Clearwater Threshers and from the Collection of AdeQ Historical Archives.*

Joel Adamson served as a pitcher for the Clearwater Phillies in 1991 and 1992. He was acquired as the Phillies' seventh selection in the 1990 June draft. Note the new ball cap of the Clearwater Phillies worn from 1992 to 2003. *Courtesy Philadelphia Phillies and Clearwater Threshers and from the Collection of AdeQ Historical Archives.*

In 1993 the Clearwater Phillies became champions of the 1993 Florida State League. In the finals, the Phillies defeated the St. Lucie Mets, three games to one. The team is pictured with their championship trophy on the cover of the 1994 Clearwater Phillies score card. In addition the team celebrated its tenth anniversary. *Courtesy Philadelphia Phillies and Clearwater Threshers and from the Collection of AdeQ Historical Archives.*

During the playing season, there are numerous entertainers that make the fans' experiences more memorable. Seen here is baseball comedian Max Patkin, the Clown Prince of Baseball, who entertained the crowds at Jack Russell Stadium with his antics during the 1980s. *From the Collection of AdeQ Historical Archives.*

Philbert was one of the earliest mascots of the Clearwater Phillies during the late 1980s and early 1990s. *Courtesy Philadelphia Phillies and Clearwater Threshers and from the Collection of AdeQ Historical Archives.*

A team photo of the 1995 Clearwater Phillies. Among the players are Scott Rolen, and the manager at the time was Don McCormick. One of the coaches pictured is Greg Legg, who would later be the manager of the Clearwater Threshers in 2005. *Courtesy Philadelphia Phillies and Clearwater Threshers and from the Collection of AdeQ Historical Archives.*

A scene at the Clearwater Phillies dugout during the 2003 season, their last at Jack Russell Stadium. *Courtesy Philadelphia Phillies and Clearwater Threshers.*

A score card from 2003 showing the Clearwater Phillies official mascot, Phil E. Phox. He was a regular at Clearwater games between 1996 and 2003. *Courtesy Philadelphia Phillies and Clearwater Threshers and from the Collection of AdeQ Historical Archives.*

THRESHERS
abc ACTION NEWS
CLEARWAT
SCHMIDT
20

During the fall of 2003, Mike Schmidt was named the new manager of the minor league team that is now renamed the Clearwater Threshers. These views show Schmidt accepting his position as manager of the team at Bright House Networks Field while it was still under construction. The Philadelphia Phillies and their minor league affiliate moved to the new facility from Jack Russell Stadium and began playing at their new facility with the 2004 season. *Courtesy Philadelphia Phillies and Clearwater Threshers.*

Schmidt is seen among his players during their inaugural season at Bright House Networks Field in 2004. The team is wearing their distinctive home uniforms. *Courtesy Philadelphia Phillies and Clearwater Threshers.*

Safety Harbor
RESORT & SPA
PHILIPS
BALL
STRIKE
Shephard's
Here's the pitch!
415-5665
JEFF HART
Best Western
Sea Wake Resort Clearwater Beach
ADVANTAGE
Tire & Auto

Players of the Clearwater Threshers wearing their batting uniforms, in which the team's logo on the jerseys and caps shows the shark grasping a baseball bat rather than a baseball. *Courtesy Philadelphia Phillies and Clearwater Threshers.*

On June 18, 2005, the Florida State League All-Star Game was held at Bright House Networks Field. Players from teams from all parts of the Florida State League gathered to play against each other. *Photo by the author.*

The Clearwater Threshers' Tim Moss (far right) among players from the Tampa Yankees, Detroit Tigers and the Fort Myers Miracles during the 2005 Florida State League All-Star Game in Bright House Networks Field, Clearwater, Florida. *Photo by the author.*

After two seasons, the Clearwater Threshers introduced their new mascot, Phinley the Shark, during the first home game at Bright House Networks Field on April 6, 2006. He quickly became a popular celebrity at the Threshers home games. *Photo by the author.*

A canine Threshers fan watching a game during Bark at the Ballpark night at Bright House Networks Field in 2006. Like their parent organization, the Clearwater Threshers are strongly involved in the community and with charities. Bark at the Ballpark is an event used to benefit the Humane Society of Pinellas County. *Photo by the author.*

A scene from behind the Threshers' dugout during a game against the Sarasota Reds, 2006. *Photo by the author.*

The Clearwater Threshers are unique among baseball teams in their use of uniforms, especially for special causes. Seen here is a Threshers player wearing a pink jersey in honor of Breast Cancer Awareness night on August 18, 2006. As a means of donating funds for the cause, the jerseys were auctioned off and presented to the winners after the game. The Threshers in past years have had uniquely designed jerseys made for events such as for the Fourth of July (2005) and for Tropical Paradise Night (2006). *Photo by the author.*

Players from the Clearwater Threshers during workout prior to a game at Bright House Networks Field, 2006. *Photo by the author.*

Hertz
VINCENZO'S
TAMPA'S FASTEST GROWING HOME BUILDER
SYSCO
CAY CLUB
THE TAMPA TRIBUNE
27
19

A New Era in the Twenty-first Century

The Philadelphia Phillies had an instant hit with the opening of Bright House Networks Field in 2004, as the ballpark opened to wide acclaim. The praise is deserved, as the new ballpark is one of the more charming and comfortable facilities in all of spring training.

Bright House Networks Field is built on a familiar model: a concourse rings the entire field, with a two-story grandstand and berm seating in the outfield. One is never too far away from the playing field at any time. The stadium is of a Spanish architectural style, where the fans enter through the main concourse that is located above the seats. It is unlike most other stadiums of the Grapefruit League where one must enter through tunnels to get to the main seating area. Bright House Networks Field has seven thousand seats with seventy-five seats around the massive Tiki Bar on the left field line, which dwarfed the old one at Jack Russell Stadium. Below it is a tiered section of about one hundred high barstools that face the field. One of the unique features is a berm that goes completely around the outfield, with the bullpens cut into the left field berm. One can stand on the berm and get a closer glimpse of the pitchers warming up in the bullpen.

In addition, Bright House Networks Field features some cozy spaces for groups. The legendary Tiki Bar—perfect for cool cocktails on a hot day—is set up in left field, while there's patio seating (chairs surrounding a patio table) down the left field line. Philadelphia residents won't go hungry: Philly cheese steaks and Yuengling beer are both on sale. Speaking of beer, there is a "Beers of the World" stand that features well over forty different types of beer. For children there is a playground and moonwalk.

There are numerous events that help fans appreciate the public relations staff and the teams that they represent. Most are fundraising events that are for good causes, such as Bark at the Ballpark for the Humane Society of Pinellas and the previously mentioned Breast Cancer Awareness Night, where the Threshers wear pink uniforms! In addition, the Threshers hold a weeklong Baseball Camp at the spring training facilities for youths during the summer. This gives boys and girls the opportunity to meet real ballplayers up close and personal, as well as learn valuable skills that they can utilize in playing the great American pastime. Finally, the ballpark is easy to find: it's next to U.S. Highway 19—a major highway in Clearwater and convenient to get to from anywhere in the Tampa–St. Petersburg area. In addition, Bright House Networks Field is also close to Dunedin, the spring home of the Toronto Blue Jays and their affiliate Dunedin Blue Jays.

On a sad note, Paul "The Pope" Owens, the former Phillies manager instrumental in the building of Clearwater's Carpenter Field in 1967, died at the age of seventy-nine on December 26, 2003. Within two weeks, former Phillies star Tug McGraw, age fifty-nine, succumbed to brain cancer on January 5, 2004. Larry Shenk reported, "Their uniform jerseys—Owens (#5) and McGraw (#45)—hung in the new Phillies clubhouse at Bright House Networks Field during spring training and will also be displayed in the clubhouse at Citizens Bank Park during this Season. The team will also honor Pope and Tug on their uniforms throughout the 2004 regular season."

The Philadelphia Phillies won the first game at the new park, 5–1, over the New York Yankees on March 4, 2004, before 8,205 fans, a Clearwater attendance record. George Steinbrenner, owner of the Yankees, described Bright House Networks Field: "It's the nicest I've seen. I love Legends Field [the Yankees home in Tampa], but this place is beautiful." Vicente Padilla threw the first pitch at the field at 1:11 p.m. A single by Marlon Byrd in the first inning was the ballpark's first hit, and the first run was from Byrd on a sac fly by Jim Thome during the first inning. The first homerun was from Jimmy Rollins in the third inning.

Bobby Abreu (Phillies), Miguel Cabrera (Marlins), Melvin Mora (Orioles) and Omar Vizquel (Giants) were among the stars on the Venezuela team who played an exhibition game in Clearwater on March 4, 2006, prior to competing in the sixteen-team World Baseball Classic in April. The exhibition game was played at Bright House Networks Field at 1:05 p.m.

The first game for Venezuela in the World Baseball Classic was played at 1:00 p.m., Tuesday, March 7, versus the Dominican Republic at the ballpark at Disney's Wide World of Sports Complex in Orlando. Among the players on the thirty-five-man roster were pitchers Giovanni Carrara, Gustavo Chacin, Kelvim Escobar, Freddy Garcia, Jorge Julio, Johan Santana, Carlos Silva, Carlos Zambrano and Victor Zambrano; catchers Henry Blanco, Ramon Hernandez and Victor Martinez; infielders Edgardo Alfonzo, Luis Gonzalez, Carlos Guillen, Melvin Mora, Tomas Perez, Marco Scutaro and Omar Vizquel; outfielders Bobby Abreu, Miguel Cabrera, Endy Chavez, Magglio Ordonez and Juan Rivera; and Manager Luis Sojo.

Opie Cheek is considered a fixture associated with the Philadelphia Phillies and the Clearwater Threshers for nearly two decades. Simply known as Opie by his fans, he began his job as groundskeeper in 1987. Within two years he would become the turf manager for Jack Russell Stadium. Over the decades, Jack Russell Stadium had been recognized as one of the best-kept fields in the Grapefruit League. Cheek had been named Sports Turf Manager of the Year in the Florida State League in 2004 and 2005. His ground crew was also recognized in 2004 and 2005 when they won the Florida State League Sports Turf Crew award. This award was initiated in 1990 and selection is made by the field managers and pitching coaches of each team in the Florida State League. The five awards are Best Overall Award, Municipality Award and three commendation certificates. A cult of sorts has been formed around Opie. In 2005 Opie Cheek was honored with a promotional handout of bobbleheads in the caricature of him as part of the "Opie Cuts Grass" campaign, which included a comical skit and appearance by Opie in a television commercial. The following year Opie fans were able to purchase headgear in the shape of a clipped head of grass, and a barbecue stand honoring Opie opened within the stands of Bright House Networks Field. The year 2007 will mark Opie's twentieth anniversary with the Philadelphia Phillies and the Clearwater Phillies/Threshers.

In recent years, crowd attendance has been setting records at Bright House Networks Field. A spring training record of 9,893 was set on Sunday, March 26, 2006, with the Philadelphia Phillies versus the Boston Red Sox. The Clearwater Threshers set a single game attendance record of 8,216 on Friday, June 30, 2006, at Bright House Networks Field versus the Lakeland Tigers. The crowd surpassed the previous record of 7,027 set on June 18, 2004. Through 36 games during the 2006 season, Clearwater has notched an attendance of 85,699 and an average of 2,381 per game—10 behind the Florida State League lead. By August 2006, in their sixtieth home opening out of a scheduled seventy, the Clearwater Threshers of the Florida State League set a new record for single-season attendance on Friday night. An announced crowd of 3,276 witnessed the Western Division–lead Clearwater Threshers best the Dunedin Blue Jays by a score of 6–3. The total sent the Threshers 2006 attendance to a record 137,462 fans, the most ever in a single season. The Phillies began play in Clearwater as the Clearwater Phillies in 1985. The previous mark of 135,073 was set in 2004, the first year the Threshers began play at Bright House Networks Field. The all-time attendance record was set at 159,067 by the end of the 2006 season.

"It is a tribute to our hardworking Clearwater staff, and a beautiful ballpark, but most importantly it reflects on the fans here in Clearwater and Pinellas County," said John Timberlake, Threshers general manager. Timberlake also attributed the increase in numbers to the team on the field: "We have been fortunate in that the Phillies organization has provided a quality product on the field and [Manager] Greg Legg and his coaches have done an outstanding job this year…We have been blessed with great weather this year. If that continues, with the special events we still have upcoming, we have a chance to really do some special numbers." He added, "It's rewarding to our staff because we started last fall with a great game plan and have been able to follow it through. But the real difference is the fans. They have just been outstanding."

In fact, for the second consecutive season, Minor League Baseball established a new all-time attendance record, as 176 teams in 15 leagues drew a total of 41,333,279 fans for regular season games. Despite the loss of several openings due to Hurricane Katrina, 2005 attendance increased by 1,445,523 (3.6 percent), breaking the 2004 total of 39,887,755.

The Philadelphia Phillies and the Clearwater Threshers are an important fabric of the greater Tampa Bay community and a major option for family entertainment. One can only look forward to continued success and growth.

This elaborate statue of a Phillies player of days gone by adorns the fountain in front of the field's main entrance, asserting that the Philadelphia Phillies are here to stay in Clearwater in the decades to come. *Photo by the author.*

The main entrance to Bright House Networks Field in 2006. The Spanish-style architecture fits in perfectly within the Florida landscape. *Photo by the author.*

Grand opening of Bright House Networks Field with the Philadelphia Phillies mascot, Phillie Phanatic, officiating the event. *Courtesy Philadelphia Phillies and Clearwater Threshers.*

field

The first pitch at the new stadium during an inaugural game between the Philadelphia Phillies and the New York Yankees on March 4, 2004. *Courtesy Philadelphia Phillies and Clearwater Threshers.*

GREY GOOSE
Times
Bud
BUD LIGHT
Coca-Cola
bright house field
INAUGURAL GAME
Thursday March 4, 2004
1:05pm
Philadelphia Phillies
vs.
New York Yankees
Spring Training

Bobby Abreu at bat during a game in Bright House Networks Field during the 2004 spring training season. Following the charitable and philanthropic traditions of the Phillies, Abreu would purchase $10,000 of tickets to most Friday evening games for children in his "Abreu's Amigos" program in 2003 and 2004. In the program the children would receive jerseys, coupons for concessions and the chance to meet Bobby on the field during batting practice. *Courtesy Philadelphia Phillies and Clearwater Threshers.*

Phillie Phanatic gathers up support for the home team from the top of the Philadelphia Phillies dugout during a spring training game at Bright House Networks Field, 2004. *Courtesy Philadelphia Phillies and Clearwater Threshers.*

Jim Thome wears the Philadelphia Phillies inaugural season patch and the Paul Owens–Tug McGraw memorial patch on the sleeve of his jersey during the 2004 baseball season. The jerseys of Paul "Pope" Owens and Tug McGraw hung for a time at the Carpenter Training Complex as a memorial during spring training before being sent back to Philadelphia. *Courtesy Philadelphia Phillies and Clearwater Threshers.*

A spring training program from 2005 showing Jim Thome at bat. On his jersey's sleeve is a commemorative patch of Philadelphia's Veterans Stadium. *Courtesy Philadelphia Phillies and Clearwater Threshers and from the Collection of AdeQ Historical Archives.*

Jimmy Rollins at bat, 2004. *Courtesy Philadelphia Phillies and Clearwater Threshers.*

Since 1948 the Phillies maintained a wonderful relationship with the city of Clearwater. As part of their long-standing relationship, the Philadelphia Phillies have given back to the community of Clearwater in many ways. Seen here is right-handed pitcher Amaury Telemarco greeting children at Bright House Networks Field. The Phillies host youth organizations at spring training workouts at the Carpenter Complex. Clearwater's Paul B. Stephens School's Special Olympics teams and the Boys and Girls Clubs of Clearwater have been guests of the Phillies at their workouts in recent years. *Courtesy Philadelphia Phillies and Clearwater Threshers.*

Philadelphia Phillies pitcher Randy Wolf visiting young children in Clearwater. Wolf served as a spokesman for the Children's Miracle Network in 2003 and 2004, purchasing over $6,000 in tickets each year for CMN and the children's families. In addition, he has taken part in the "Baseballers Against Drugs" free baseball clinic for inner city kids. *Courtesy Philadelphia Phillies and Clearwater Threshers.*

Each year, the Phillies and Clearwater Threshers host a fun-filled carnival for kids and adults at Bright House Networks Field. During Phanfest, players sign balls and have their photos taken with their fans. Tours of the field are given. In support of youth baseball former Philadelphia Phillies pitcher Dickie Noles, pictured here, has made appearances at several area youth baseball league opening day ceremonies. Additionally, the Phillies have donated thousands of dollars raised at the annual Phanfest to Clearwater's T-ball organization. *Courtesy Philadelphia Phillies and Clearwater Threshers.*

The playing field of Bright House Networks Field as seen from stands alongside of left field. *Photo by the author.*

Over the years, Field Supervisor Opie Cheek has become a celebrity of sorts and has even garnered his own fan club. Recognized as one of the best groundskeepers in both the Major and minor leagues, he has been awarded numerous honors. In 2005 he was honored by having a caricature bobblehead made of him and handed out to the fans during a Threshers home game. *Photo by the author.*

A band playing behind the Tiki Bar at Bright House Networks Field. *Photo by the author.*

There is almost always happy hour on Wednesday, regardless if there is a game or not. The Tiki Bar is unique among spring training stadiums in the Grapefruit League and has proven quite popular by those who attend the games of the Philadelphia Phillies and the Clearwater Threshers. *Photo by the author.*

The greatest thing that sets the Clearwater Threshers apart from other baseball teams is their relationship with their fans. Most of the players make themselves available to meet up with fans of all sizes and sign autographs. Seen here are autograph-seeking kids throwing balls over the dugout to the players during a lull in a game. Manager Greg Legg makes a point to acknowledge fans and have small talks with them prior to and after the games. *Photo by the author.*

Acknowledgements

Without the enthusiastic support of the Philadelphia Phillies and the Clearwater Threshers Baseball Clubs this research would not have been a possibility; thanks especially to Jason Adams, Carrie Jenkins-Adams, Amanda Warner and Chris Guckian for their assistance.

In addition, I would like to thank the following whose assistance has made this book possible: Wes Singletary, Florida State Archives; Bruce Graetz, Museum of Florida History; Vincent Luisi, director, Dunedin Historical Museum; Don Spivey, the Pinellas County Historical Museum; Mike Sanders, Clearwater Historical Society; the National Baseball Library, Cooperstown, New York; and the Baseball Hall of Fame, Cooperstown, New York.

Appendix I
Clearwater Baseball in Brief

I.

The following Major League Baseball teams have used Clearwater as their base for spring training: the Brooklyn Dodgers, 1923–32 and 1936–40; the Cleveland Indians, 1942 and 1946; and the Philadelphia Phillies, 1947–present.

II.

The Philadelphia Phillies have held spring training in the following locations:

1901	Philadelphia, Pennsylvania
1902	Washington, North Carolina
1903	Richmond, Virginia
1904	Savannah, Georgia
1905	Augusta, Georgia
1906–08	Savannah, Georgia
1909–10	Southern Pines, North Carolina
1911	Birmingham, Alabama
1912	Hot Springs, Arkansas

1913	Southern Pines, North Carolina
1914	Wilmington, North Carolina
1915–18	St. Petersburg, Florida
1919	Charlotte, North Carolina
1920	Birmingham, Alabama
1921	Gainesville, Florida
1922–24	Leesburg, Florida
1925–27	Bradenton, Florida
1928–37	Winter Haven, Florida
1938	Biloxi, Mississippi
1939	New Braunfels, Texas
1940–42	Miami Beach, Florida
1943	Hershey, Pennsylvania
1944–45	Wilmington, Delaware
1946	Miami Beach, Florida
1947–present	Clearwater, Florida

The Philadelphia Phillies have been training in Clearwater since 1947 and at Jack Russell Stadium from 1955 through 2003. Since 2004 the Phillies' new spring training home has been Bright House Networks Field along U.S. Highway 19.

III.

The following Minor League Baseball teams have called Clearwater home: Clearwater Pelicans, Florida State League (D), 1924; Clearwater Phillies, Florida State League (A), 1985–2003, renamed Clearwater Threshers, Florida State League (A), 2004–Present; Gulf Coast Phillies, Gulf Coast League (R), 1999–present.

Appendix II
Statistics of the Clearwater Phillies/Threshers, 1985–2006

1985 Clearwater Phillies
Record: 69–72 / .489
Fourth in Florida State League Western Division
Manager: Ramon Aviles
Stadium: Jack Russell Memorial Stadium
Playoffs: Did not qualify
Attendance: 44,081

1986 Clearwater Phillies
Record: 63–74 / .460
Third in Florida State League Western Division
Manager: Ron Clark
Stadium: Jack Russell Memorial Stadium
Playoffs: Did not qualify
Attendance: 53,824

1987 Clearwater Phillies
Record: 66–70 / .485
Third in Florida State League Western Division
Manager: Roly DeArmas
Stadium: Jack Russell Memorial Stadium
Playoffs: Did not qualify
Attendance: 55,370

1988 Clearwater Phillies
Record: (1) 25–44 / .362
Fourth in Florida State League Western Division
(2) 27–42 / .391
Fourth in Florida State League Western Division
Manager: Granny Hamner
Stadium: Jack Russell Memorial Stadium
Playoffs: Did not qualify
Attendance: 50,456

1989 Clearwater Phillies
Record: (1) 34–36 / .486
Fourth in Florida State League Western Division
(2) 23–43 / .348
Fifth in Florida State League Western Division
Manager: Glenn Gulliver
Stadium: Jack Russell Memorial Stadium
Playoffs: Did not qualify
Attendance: 68,591

1990 Clearwater Phillies
Record: (1) 23–46 / .333
Fifth in Florida State League Western Division
(2) 27–41 / .397
Fifth in Florida State League Western Division
Manager: Lee Elia
Stadium: Jack Russell Memorial Stadium
Playoffs: Did not qualify
Attendance: 91,040

1991 Clearwater Phillies
Record: (1) 42–23 / .646
First in Florida State League Western Division
(2) 39–26 / .600
First in Florida State League Western Division
Manager: Lee Elia
Stadium: Jack Russell Memorial Stadium
Playoffs: Clearwater defeated St. Lucie 2 games to 1; West Palm Beach defeated Clearwater 2 games to 0 to win Florida State League Championship
Attendance: 82,631

1992 Clearwater Phillies
Record: (1) 38–31 / .551
Second in Florida State League Western Division
(2) 37–28 / .569
Second in Florida State League Western Division
Manager: Bill Dancy
Stadium: Jack Russell Memorial Stadium
Playoffs: Clearwater defeated Dunedin 2 games to 0; Lakeland defeated Clearwater 2 games to 0 in the semifinals
Attendance: 91,834

1993 Clearwater Phillies
Record: (1) 44–24 / .647
First in Florida State League Western Division
(2) 31–36 / .463
Fifth in Florida State League Western Division
Manager: Bill Dancy
Stadium: Jack Russell Memorial Stadium
Playoffs: Clearwater defeated Charlotte 2 games to 1; Clearwater defeated St. Lucie 3 games to 1 to win FSL Championship
Attendance: 86,508

1994 Clearwater Phillies
Record: (1) 36–33 / .522
Fifth in Florida State League Western Division
(2) 36–29 / .554
Third in Florida State League Western Division
Manager: Don McCormack
Stadium: Jack Russell Memorial Stadium
Playoffs: Did not qualify
Attendance: 82,494

1995 Clearwater Phillies
Record: (1) 38–32 / .543
Second in Florida State League Western Division
(2) 41–27 / .603
Second in Florida State League Western Division
Manager: Don McCormack
Stadium: Jack Russell Memorial Stadium
Playoffs: Did not qualify
Attendance: 71,761

1996 Clearwater Phillies
Record: (1) 44–26 / .629
First in Florida State League Western Division
(2) 41–21 / .603
Second in Florida State League Western Division
Manager: Al LeBoeuf
Stadium: Jack Russell Memorial Stadium
Playoffs: Clearwater defeated Tampa 2 games to none; St. Lucie defeated Clearwater 3 games to 1 to win FSL Championship
Attendance: 75,118

1997 Clearwater Phillies
Record: (1) 31–38 / .449
Seventh in Florida State League Western Division
(2) 39–30 / .565
Fourth in Florida State League Western Division
Manager: Roy Majtyka
Stadium: Jack Russell Memorial Stadium
Playoffs: Did not qualify
Attendance: 97,687

1998 Clearwater Phillies
Record: (1) 42–28 / .600
Third in Florida State League Western Division
(2) 40–30 / .571
Second in Florida State League Western Division
Manager: Bill Dancy
Stadium: Jack Russell Memorial Stadium
Playoffs: Did not qualify
Attendance: 73,300

1999 Clearwater Phillies
Record: (1) 46–23 / .667
First in Florida State League Western Division
(2) 31–36 / .463
Seventh in Florida State League Western Division
Manager: Bill Dancy
Stadium: Jack Russell Memorial Stadium
Playoffs: Dunedin defeated Clearwater 2 games to 1
Attendance: 70,147

2000 Clearwater Phillies
Record: (1) 37–33 / .529
Fourth in Florida State League Western Division
(2) 27–38 / .415
Seventh in Florida State League Western Division
Manager: Ken Oberkfell
Stadium: Jack Russell Memorial Stadium
Playoffs: Did not qualify
Attendance: 83,895

2001 Clearwater Phillies
Record: (1) 32–35 / .478
Third in Florida State League Western Division
(2) 36–34 / .514
Fourth in Florida State League Western Division
Manager: Ramon Aviles
Stadium: Jack Russell Memorial Stadium
Playoffs: Did not qualify
Attendance: 76,406

Appendix II

2002 Clearwater Phillies
Record: 57–79 / .419
Sixth in Florida State League Western Division
Managers: John Morris, Roly DeArmas
Stadium: Jack Russell Memorial Stadium
Playoffs: Did not qualify
Attendance: 78,459

2003 Clearwater Phillies
Record: 72–61 / .541
Third in Florida State League West Division
Manager: Roly DeArmas
Stadium: Jack Russell Memorial Stadium
Playoffs: Did not qualify
Attendance: 63,655

2004 Clearwater Threshers
Record: 55–81 / .404
Fifth in Florida State League West Division
Manager: Mike Schmidt
Stadium: Bright House Networks Field
Playoffs: Did not qualify
Attendance: 135,082

2005 Clearwater Threshers
Record: 41–95 / .301
Sixth in Florida State League Western Division
Manager: Greg Legg
Stadium: Bright House Networks Field
Playoffs: Did not qualify
Attendance: 130,446

2006 Clearwater Threshers
Record: 67–72
Manager: Greg Legg
Stadium: Bright House Networks Field
Playoffs: Did not qualify
Attendance: 159,067

Bibliography

Adams, Jason. Personal correspondence. August 16, 2005.

Borsvold, David. *Cleveland Indians: The Cleveland Press Years, 1920–1982*. Charleston, SC: Arcadia Publishing, 2003.

Byrd, Alan. *Florida Spring Training: Your Guide to Touring the Grapefruit League*. Branford, CT: The Intrepid Traveler, 2005.

de Quesada, Alejandro M. *Baseball in Tampa Bay*. Charleston, SC: Arcadia Publishing, 2000.

———. *Ybor City*. Charleston, SC: Arcadia Publishing, 1999.

de Quesada, Alejandro M., and Vincent Luisi. *Pinellas County*. Charleston, SC: Arcadia Publishing, 1998.

Dewey, Donald, and Nicholas Acocella. *Total Ballclubs: The Ultimate Book of Baseball Teams*. Toronto: Sport Media Publishing, 2005.

Eckhouse, Morris. *Legends of the Tribe: An Illustrated History of the Cleveland Indians*. Dallas, TX: Taylor Publishing Company, 2000.

Filichia, Peter. *Professional Baseball Franchises: From the Abbeville Athletics to the Zanesville Indians*. New York: Facts On File, 1993.

Florida Spring Training Guide 2006. Tallahassee: Florida Sports Foundation, 2006.

Florida State League. *2005 Florida State League Media Guide and Record Book*. Daytona: Florida State League, 2005.

Gordon, Robert. Legends of the Philadelphia Phillies. Champaign, IL: Sports Publishing, 2005.

Inside the Clearwater Threshers blog. http://threshersbaseball.blogspot.com/

Jenkins, Carrie. Personal correspondence. August 12 and 16, 2005.

Jordan, David M. *Occasional Glory: The History of the Philadelphia Phillies*. Jefferson, NC: McFarland & Company, 2002.

Kraus, Rebecca S. *Minor League Baseball: Community Building Through Hometown Sports*. New York: The Haworth Press, 2003.

Lewis, Allen. "Philadelphia–Clearwater: '47–'86." *Phillies Spring Training Program*. Clearwater, 1996.

Looney, Jack. *Now Batting Number…The Mystique, Superstition, and Lore of Baseball's Uniform Numbers*. New York: Black Dog & Leventhal Publishers, 2006.

McCarthy, Kevin M. *Baseball in Florida*. Sarasota, FL: Pineapple Press, 1996.

McNeil, William F. *The Dodgers Encyclopedia*. Jefferson, NC: McFarland & Company, 2003.

Montville, Leigh. *The Big Bam: The Life and Times of Babe Ruth*. New York: Doubleday, 2006.

National Baseball Hall of Fame and Museum 2006 Yearbook. Cooperstown, NY: National Baseball Hall of Fame and Museum, 2006.

"New Spring Home." *Phillies 2004*, 96–97.

Okkonen, Marc. *Baseball Uniforms of the 20th Century*. New York: Sterling Publishing Company, Inc., 1991.

Orodenker, Richard, ed. *The Phillies Reader*. Philadelphia: Temple University Press, 2005.

Pahigian, Joshua R. *Spring Training Handbook: A Comprehensive Guide to the Ballparks of the Grapefruit and Cactus Leagues*. Jefferson, NC: McFarland & Company, 2005.

Pedersen, Paul. *Build It and They Will Come: The Arrival of the Tampa Bay Devil Rays*. Stuart: Florida Sports Press, 1997.

Philadelphia Phillies 2006 Media Guide. Philadelphia: Phillies Public Relations Office, March 2006.

Purdy, Dennis. *The Team by Team Encyclopedia of Major League Baseball*. New York: Workman Publishing Company, 2006.

Putnam, Bob. "New manager's job: turn around Clearwater Phillies." *St. Petersburg Times*, June 28, 2002.

Roberts, Robin, and C. Paul Rogers III. *My Life in Baseball*. Chicago: Triumph Books, 2003.

Rossi, John P. *The 1964 Phillies: The Story of Baseball's Most Memorable Collapse*. Jefferson, NC: McFarland & Company, 2005.

Sanders, Mike. "Clearwater, a fertile ground for baseball's spring training." *Tampa Tribune*, March 3, 1996.

Schmidt, Mike. *Clearing the Bases: Juiced Players, Monster Salaries, Sham Records, and a Hall of Famer's Search for the Soul of Baseball*. New York: HarperCollins Publishers, 2006.

Schneider, Russell. *Cleveland Indians Encyclopedia*. Champaign, IL: Sports Publishing, 2004.

Shaughnessy, Dan, and Stan Grossfeld. *Spring Training: Baseball's Early Season.* New York: Houghton Mifflin, 2003.

Shenk, Larry. "Ballpark Bill." *Phillies 2004*, 2004: 18–19.

———. "In Memory of Two Phillies Icons." *Phillies 2004*, 2004: 66–67.

———, ed. *Philadelphia Phillies Official Yearbook.* Elmont, NY: University Sports Publications Co., 2004.

Simpson, Allen. *Baseball America Directory 2005.* Durham, SC: Baseball America Inc., 2005.

Singletary, Wes. *Al Lopez: The Life of Baseball's El Señor.* Jefferson, NC: McFarland & Company, 1999.

———. *Florida's First Big League Baseball Players: A Narrative History.* Charleston, SC: The History Press, 2006.

Stang, Mark. *Indians Illustrated: 100 Years of Cleveland Indians Photos.* Wilmington, OH: Orange Frazer Press, 2000.

Stout, Glenn. *The Dodgers: 120 Years of Dodgers Baseball.* New York: Houghton Mifflin, 2004.

Sweet, Ozzie. *The Boys of Spring: Timeless Portraits from the Grapefruit League, 1947–2005.* Toronto: Sports Media Publishing, 2005.

Westcott, Rich. "Phillies Ballparks: Nothing Left but the Memories..." *Phillies 2004*, 2004: 21–26.

———. *Phillies Essential: Everything You Needed to Know to be a Fan*! Chicago: Triumph Books, 2006.

———. *Tales from the Phillies Dugout: A Collection of the Greatest Philadelphia Phillies Stories Ever Told.* Champaign, IL: Sports Publishing, 2003.

Westcott, Ric, and Frank Bilovsky. *The Phillies Encyclopedia.* Philadelphia: Temple University Press, 2004.

Whittingham, Richard. *Illustrated History of the Dodgers.* Chicago: Triumph Books, 2005.